Healing
Our Broken
Village

OTHER BOOKS BY
DR. FREDERICK D. HAYNES, III

Soul Fitness

*Blow the Trumpet in Zion! Global Vision and
Action for the 21st Century Black Church*
(Co-Editor)

*Sound the Trumpet Again! More Messages to
Empower African American Men*
(Contributor)

HEALING
OUR BROKEN
VILLAGE

DR. FREDERICK D. HAYNES, III

HEALING OUR BROKEN VILLAGE

Cover Design by Jack Akana, Graphic Specialist,
Friendship-West Baptist Church, Dallas, TX

© Copyright 2008

SAINT PAUL PRESS, DALLAS, TEXAS

First Printing, 2008

The Bible quotations in this volume are from the New International and King James Versions of the Bible.

The name SAINT PAUL PRESS and its logo are registered as a trademark in the U.S. patent office.

ISBN: 0-9817520-1-2
ISBN-13: 978-0-9817520-1-3

Printed in the U.S.A.

DEDICATION

This book is dedicated to the village that has nurtured and raised me:

Teachers: *Homoselle Davis, Dr. John Mangrum, and Dr. Harry S. Wright.*

Mentors: *The late Dr. Manuel L. Scott, Sr.; The late Dr. Frederick G. Sampson; The late Dr. E. V. Hill; Dr. Jeremiah A. Wright, Jr.; Dr. Zan W. Holmes, Jr.; Dr. Charles G. Adams; and Dr. Amos C. Brown.*

This village has inspired me to dream, encouraged me through my darkest moments, and facilitated my growth and sense of calling.

—Dr. Frederick D. Haynes, III

CONTENTS

Introduction..15

1. Cleared for Take-Off But Refusing to Fly................19

2. My Family Is A Hot Mess...................................39

3. You Were Born To Blow Up.................................57

4. Sexual Healing...73

5. Why Is Loving You Hurting Me?...........................95

6. There's Some Music We Just Can't Dance To............117

7. What's Up With The Down-Low?..........................137

8. Aren't You Sick Of This?................................155

9. Over My Dead Body......................................175

10. Don't Set Your Queen Up To Be A "Ho"..................193

11. What Happens When a Black Man Goes Home...219

ACKNOWLEDGEMENTS

First and foremost, I wish to thank God for placing this burden upon my heart to help bring healing to our broken village—the African-American community.

Second, I wish to thank my dutiful staff for having the vision to put this important book together.

May God richly bless each of you for your dedicated work on this project.

Introduction

We have all heard the African proverb, "It takes a village to raise a child." That is true. But, if we have a broken village, we cannot raise whole children. Generally speaking, the African-American village, or community of today, is broken. When our village is broken that indicates that there are broken people in our village, and when we have broken people, we have broken families, a broken economy, broken churches, and broken schools.

Some of our fathers are refusing to take their God-given responsibilities to lead, guide, and direct their families under God's direction. Many others are handcuffed by the criminal justice system or dysfunctional relationships with their "baby mama's."

Some of our mothers have had to take on the role of being the mother and the father to their children, many, through no fault of their own.

Because of this dysfunction, our children are caught

in the middle—confused and conflicted—not knowing which way to go in life.

The families of our village are dealing with their individual internal issues which are getting in the way of what God wants to do to bring about restoration to our broken village.

The village is also under attack by the forces of racism and oppression. The criminal justice system and our nation's public schools seemingly have constructed an invisible, but real, school yard to prison cell pipeline. Economic apartheid cripples the development of African-American communities, often mired in poverty.

This book is an attempt to look at and to address, under the power and authority of God's Word, the issues that have left us broken as a people and thus, broken as a village.

My prayer is that God will make us more aware of the problems in our broken village, and place upon our hearts a desire, with His help, to strive to put our broken village back together for His glory!

—Dr. Frederick D. Haynes, III
Friendship-West Baptist Church
Dallas, Texas

CLEARED FOR TAKE-OFF BUT REFUSING TO FLY

The angel of the LORD came and sat down under the oak in Ophrah that belonged to Joash the Abiezrite, where his son Gideon was threshing wheat in a winepress to keep it from the Midianites. When the angel of the LORD appeared to Gideon, he said, "The LORD is with you, mighty warrior." "But sir," Gideon replied, "if the LORD is with us, why has all this happened to us? Where are all his wonders that our fathers told us about when they said, 'Did not the LORD bring us up out of Egypt?' But now the LORD has abandoned us and put us into the hand of Midian." The LORD turned to him and said, "Go in the strength you have and save Israel out of Midian's hand. Am I not sending you?" "But Lord," Gideon asked, "how can I save Israel? My clan is the weakest in Manasseh, and I am the least in my family." The LORD answered, "I will be with you, and you will strike down all the Midianites together."

—Judges 6:11-16

Have you ever been sentenced to a prison without bars? Have you ever known the excruciating experience of being locked in a room with open doors? Have you ever found out that there was something in your way prohibiting you from getting where you desired to go, only to discover that the something that was in your way was you?

Well, every now and then, we blame other people and other things for where we are and for where we are not, only to discover that we are our own worst enemy. Our own issues internally incarcerate us and preclude us from being everything that God has divinely designed and cosmically created us to become.

I came across a sagacious story about a man who dreamt of one day flying a plane. He went through all the necessary requirements for securing his pilot's license. Can you picture him as he enrolls in flight school? Can you picture him as he passes all of his tests? Can you picture him as he practices on the simulator? Now the day has come for him to leave the classroom, to leave the simulator, and to go on a plane. He has done everything well up to this point. He has passed his tests, he has done well on the simulator, and now he is in the cockpit of the plane with his flight instructor. Picture the plane as it taxis down the runway. The man hears from the air traffic controller in the control tower that his plane has been cleared for take-off. As soon as he receives the word for clearance, he immediately becomes petrified and just sits there.

The instructor says, "Did you hear the controller in the

control tower? You know what to do now, don't you?" The man says, "Yes, I know what to do now, but I'm not going to do it." The instructor says, "What do you mean, you're not going to do it? You've been living for this moment. This is the moment that you have been dreaming about. Why is it that you are not going to do this?" And then the man says, "Well, I forgot to tell you one thing when I enrolled in this program. I am scared of heights."

This man had enrolled in the program with the intent of flying a plane, but he had an unresolved issue—this brother was afraid of heights. He had issues with going from ground level to sky level.

You may be like this brother—you are afraid of heights. The reason you are not where you could be or where you should be is not because you lack the training, it is not because you haven't handled your business; rather, it is because you have a fear of heights; you have a fear of going from the level where you are to the level where your dream is trying to take you. In other words, you have a fear of the unknown.

The bottom line is this: God has already put in you everything that you need to become all that God intends for you to become. You ought to be flying high. You ought to be a go-getter. You ought to be aspiring to go higher and to do everything that God has placed in you to do. But all too often, we allow issues in our lives to get in the way, and before we know it, we find ourselves sentenced to a prison without bars.

Is that not insightful and illuminating imagery—a prison without bars? Not only do we find ourselves oppressed by "stuff" outside of us, but all too often, we are imprisoned by issues within us. If anybody ought to relate to this, it is African-Americans, in what Dr. Maya Angelou called "these yet to be United States of America." Right after the victories of the civil rights struggle, African-Americans were poised on the parameters of the Promised Land. The night before he died, Dr. King said, "I may not get there with you. But I want you to know tonight, that we, as a people, will get to the promised land," because God had blessed him to look over from the mountain and to see that we were on our way. There we were as a people, poised on the parameter of our promises; we were about to help make this nation live up to its promise of being "one nation under God, with liberty and justice for all." But, then all of a sudden, something happened. What happened to us?

Yes, we have Oprah Winfrey and Michael Jordan who people like to point to as evidence of our success and equality in this country, but the vast majority of us still find ourselves disinherited, dispossessed, and still having to face racism. My question remains, my brothers and sisters, what happened to us?

I have discovered it hasn't always been the white folk. In

too many instances, it has been us, black folk, getting in the way of us becoming everything that God intends for us to become.

Yes, there is racism, but there is also "blackism." "Blackism" is when we find ourselves with persons who look like us, who are placed in power, with the responsibility of looking out for us, but really they are put there to control us. Understand that we have black leaders who have been propped up by our enemies to control us.

Allow me to divert a little here: How can you preach prosperity and have a huge mega-church, but around your mega-church you have poor folk who are not benefiting from the prosperity in your message? In too many instances we have had those among us who have been sent to control us, and then to make matters worse, there are those of us who have allowed what is in us to get in the way of what God wants to accomplish with us.

Now, let's use the story of Gideon in the Bible to help us understand some of the issues that we as black people are facing. From our text, we understand that Gideon also had some serious issues.

GIDEON HAD ISSUES WITH GOD

Judges 6:13 says: *"But sir,"* Gideon replied, *"if the LORD is with us, why has all this happened to us? Where are all his wonders that our fathers told us about when they said, 'Did not the LORD bring us up out of Egypt?' But now the LORD has abandoned us and put us into the hand of Midian.*" Even after the angel of God greets Gideon with a great salutation, *"The LORD is with you, mighty warrior,"* Gideon bursts out with his complaint in response. Gideon says, "If God is for us, why has all this happened to us?" May I stop right there? Because I appreciate Gideon's honesty. Gideon says, "Angel, I have some issues with God."

If you and I are honest, every now and then, when stuff hurts enough, we have some issues with God, too. It is not like we wake up every morning clear, confident, comforted, and convinced about what God is up to. Some days, I don't know what God is up to. Some days, I don't know where God is. Some days, I disagree with God's plan for my life. I hope you have developed enough maturity in your faith to know that it is really all right to say, "I have issues with God." God is not scared of you. God is not intimidated by your questioning Him—If God is so good, why is my situation so bad? If God is a way out of no way, then why am I stuck in the same old jacked-up situation? If God is a bridge over troubled waters, why am I drowning in my troubles? If God is a doctor Who has never lost a patient, why has my diagnosis gone from bad to worse? If God is so good, why is my situation so bad?

Well, if God is so good all the time, why has that not

translated into the realities that black folk face, day in and day out? Why is it that black folk are at the top of every negative statistical category in this world? Why is it that we are at the bottom of every poverty statistic in this world? If God is so good, why?

GIDEON HAD ISSUES WITH HIMSELF

Gideon had issues with God, but not only that: **Gideon had issues with himself.** Judges 6:11 says: ***The angel of the LORD came and sat down under the oak in Ophrah that belonged to Joash the Abiezrite, where his son Gideon was threshing wheat in a winepress to keep it from the Midianites.*** The text says that God called him, "a mighty warrior," and Gideon didn't even see it. After God told Gideon He was going to use him to save Israel, (***The LORD turned to him and said, "Go in the strength you have and save Israel out of Midian's hand. Am I not sending you?"***), Gideon says, "listen, how can I do this when I am the least of the least? My family is jacked-up, and I am the most jacked-up in my jacked-up family." You see, right there, Gideon is incarcerated in insecurity. He is locked up by low self-esteem. He doesn't think anything of himself.

Understand: life has a way of treating you according to how you feel about yourself. If you think low of yourself, then guess what, circumstances will rise up in response to how you feel about yourself. You will attract people in your life who reflect how you feel about yourself. Sisters, do you keep wondering why you attract "dogs" in your life? Well, if you don't want to keep attracting "dogs," then don't go around serving up "Kibbles and Bits."

GIDEON HAD ISSUES WITH HIS FAMILY

Gideon had issues with God, Gideon had issues with himself, and **Gideon had issues with his family.** Judges 6:15 says: ***"But Lord," Gideon asked, "how can I save Israel? My clan is the weakest in Manasseh, and I am the least in my family."*** Gideon does not even think much of his family. Have you ever felt that way? Have you ever felt like your family is the least? Is your mentality toward your family like this: I got some folk in my family I ain't too proud of, who I don't ever want to see again? The bottom line is, if you are not careful, you can have so many issues with your family that will cause you to get in the way of your receiving what God is up to in your life.

Judges 6:16 says: ***The LORD answered, "I will be with you, and you will strike down all the Midianites together."*** God is saying to Gideon, "it is going to be all right. You have been cleared to take-off. What I have to do is deal with you, and once I deal with you, I am going to give you power to rise above where you are, and when I give you power to rise above where you are, you are going to fly high." Today can be the day where we, individually or as a people, rise up to the full potential that God has invested in each and every one of us. You are meant to be more than you are. You are meant to be the head and not the tail. You are meant to be the top and not the bottom. You say, "okay, if that's the case, Pastor Haynes, show me how to deal with what is in me, so that what is in me won't get in the way of my becoming everything God intends for me to be." Let me give you three endways out of here:

I. GOD MAKES YOU CONSCIOUS OF YOUR POTENTIAL IN THE MIDST OF YOUR PREDICAMENT

First, as in the case of Gideon, **God makes you conscious of your potential in the midst of your predicament**. God lets you know greater is He that is in you than whatever is around you. If only we recognize what we have in us.

I love this text because it says: ***"The angel of the Lord comes to Gideon."*** Gideon is threshing wheat while hiding from the Midianites in a winepress. Understand, by way of context, the Midianites are now oppressing the Israelites because the Midianites have discovered a military weapon in the camel. So using the hordes of fast moving camels, the Midianites would sweep down on the nation of Israel, destroying the produce and harvest of the Israelites. Because of their military superiority, they would economically exploit them. We discover that Gideon and the Israelites find themselves economically defeated, politically drained, socially depleted, and consequently, spiritually depressed. They are in a bad situation, and now, Gideon, reflecting on the economic dysfunction and inefficiency of what is going on in their community, is threshing wheat in a winepress.

By Gideon threshing wheat in a winepress, this means he is hiding. Agriculturally, you would thresh wheat in the open, allowing the wind to blow the wheat, so that it will separate the wheat from the chaff. But because Gideon is running scared, he now says, "I am going to hide and do what I can, in spite of the economic inefficiency that is going on in the community." God appears to Gideon, and says, "Gideon, you are a mighty man of valor." Now, Gideon is scared, so much so that he is threshing wheat in a winepress, and God says, "you are a mighty man of valor."

Even though Gideon is hiding in fear, God knows the potential in Gideon and says, "I am not going to allow how your situation looks to blind you to what is in you. You don't know what is in you, yet, and because of that, I am going to speak those things that are not, as though they are, and help you to see that, indeed, you are a mighty man of valor."

The late Dr. Frederick G. Sampson blew me away in a sermon I heard him preach. Using his sanctified imagination, he talked about a conversation he had one day with a spider. Dr. Sampson said he was watching this spider on a tree outside of his home in Detroit, and while watching the spider, the wind began to blow, and as the wind blew, the spider found itself tumbling down the trunk of the tree until it hit a branch. Dr. Sampson began to feel sorry for the spider, but noticed that the spider didn't feel sorry for itself. The wind continued to blow and then, to make the spider's situation seem worse, a fly flew by the spider. After that, a butterfly floated by the spider. Dr. Sampson was upset and said to the spider, "you ought to be angry with God, spider, because you just got blown away by the wind; you were blown from one level to another level, and now a fly has flown by you, a butterfly has flown by you. Why aren't you upset?"

The spider ignored Dr. Sampson and allowed what was in it to come out. The spider attached itself to a branch that was on a level above it; the next thing you knew, it began to climb up to that level. The spider used what it already had on the inside and did not complain about what it did not have on the outside. Because the spider used what it had, it was able to soar to another level.

In elementary school, we went on a field trip to California where we saw the great Sequoia oaks. What is amazing is this: those huge oak trees come from little acorns. It blew me away when the teacher explained that with the oak trees, you can tell the history of the tree by cutting across the trunk because there are rings inside the oak tree. The rings say: "this year I experienced a drought; this year I experienced a storm; this year I was hit by lightning; this year I went through this and that."

But towering above as king of the forest, the oak tree says, "look at me now. I began as an acorn and as an acorn, I had to go through some dirt; I had to die and become something else. Everybody else had given up on me, but look at me now."

You may not look like much to other people, but God has made you an acorn and there is something in you that God has placed inside of you. You may have to go through some dirt; you may have to go through some storms; but God uses all of that for your growth.

II. GOD WILL COMMISSION YOU WITH THE PURPOSE TO BE AN ANSWER TO YOUR PROBLEM

After God makes Gideon conscious of his potential, regardless of his predicament, God speaks to Gideon, and says, "Gideon, I am going to **commission you with the purpose to be an answer to your problem**. I am going to commission you with the purpose, so you will be an answer to what ails you."

There is a lot of talk about the *Purpose Driven Life,* by Rick Warren. Everyone wants to find their purpose now. Let me tell you what your purpose is in this life: Your purpose is always within the context of God using what He has gifted you with to be an answer to a problem that is around you. In other words, God calls and creates you to be an answer. *"You are the light of the world."* Light is an answer to darkness. My purpose isn't just to get a job and make money. My purpose is always within the framework of finding out what God has uniquely made me for; and within the context of discovering that calling, God says, "I sent you here to be an answer to what ails the world."

Let me give you a few examples: "Moses, what was your calling?" "My calling was to be an answer to enslavement and Egyptian bondage." "Amos, what was your calling?" "My calling was to condemn the nation for injustice and oppression of the poor." Do you not understand that Martin Luther King, Jr., when he graduated from Boston University with a Ph.D., had been offered teaching jobs at universities up North? But Dr. King said, "no, my calling is back down South with my people." Understand that God does not always call you to do something that will make you feel comfortable; God calls you to be an answer to the problems in this world.

Jesus said, "that is why I'm here. I have been sent, not for the righteous, but to call sinners to repentance. Don't you understand that it is not those who are well who need a doctor, it is those who are sick who need a doctor?" Jesus said in Luke 4:18: *"The spirit of the Lord God is upon me because God hath anointed me to preach good news to the poor, set the captives free, heal those who are heart*

broken, open the eyes of those who are blind." You, too, are called to be an answer.

Whenever you have a sensitivity to something that is wrong, that means God wants to use you to make it right. Your calling and your purpose may be to correct the educational dysfunction that is causing schools to leave our kids behind. Your calling may be to correct the economic dysfunction that has left your community behind. But if you want to know your calling, your purpose, or your assignment, you must first understand you are anointed to be an answer.

Allow me to relate to you this story that took place during the dark days of sharecropping. This black family owned their own property with white folk living around them who were not happy about them being in the community. One of the white men, whenever his horse had to defecate, would take the horse on to the property of the black family, and he would let the horse defecate on the black family's property. He would let the horse do that every day.

One day, the son got upset and said to the father, "Daddy, why don't you do something? This is our property. You ain't got to let them do that to us." The father said, "Listen, my mama taught me that God don't like ugly, and He'll handle your enemies if you remain faithful. Son, you ain't got to fight your enemies; God will fight your battles if you just keep still."

One day, the wife of the man who kept allowing his horse to defecate on the black man's property got sick and died. The funeral home director said to the man, "We have to get some flowers for the funeral." Unknown to the white man, it was the black man who owned the flower shop. He had the best roses and the most beautiful flower frames in town.

Well, the white man was sent by the funeral home director to check out this man's flower shop. When the white man heard the name of the flower shop, he said, "That name sounds familiar." Anyway, he went there, and was surprised to see who owned the shop. It was the black brother on whose property he would take his horse to defecate. The black brother looked at him and said, "Oh, I am sorry to hear about your wife. I am going to give you a special discount on your flowers." The white man said, "Hold on, you have to explain something to me. Where did you get the money to have such a beautiful flower shop? Where did you get all of these wonderful red roses?" The black man replied, "Well, I hadn't planned on going into this business, but since you brought your horse, every day, to defecate on my property, I decided to use your horse's waste for fertilizer and it's the richest fertilizer around."

God is the only One I know Who can take the mess that other folk make and use it to bring out in you what He wants. Can you look back over your life and say, "they meant it for evil, but God meant it for good?"

Always remember that in the midst of your confusion, God has a master plan. God says, "Gideon, I'm going to send you, and you're going to defeat all of the Midianites. I'm sending you because it is all a part of My master plan." Just knowing that God has a master plan encourages me.

I won't forget when our new church facility was being built. Because I was so excited about what was going to happen, I would put on my hard hat and just walk through the place during construction. There was a lot of noise going on; it was very confusing because folk were yelling across the way at each other; big machines were breaking up concrete and moving stuff; it was dusty and just a mess. Every now and then, when some of my friends would come in from out of town, I would walk them through our facility that was still under construction, and I would point out stuff to them and say, "That's my office." "That's the pulpit." "That's the choir room." Understand, the place was just a mess, but because I had spent time with the architect, I had seen the master plan, and I already knew what was going to happen. How did I know? I knew because I had already seen the master plan and because of my relationship with the architect and the general contractor.

If you have a relationship with the Architect of the universe and the General Contractor of your life, it may look confusing right now, you may hear a lot of noise right now, you may see a lot of dust right now, but keep on walking and God will show you the right way. His Word tells us: *"And we know that all things work together for good to them that love God, to them who are the called according to his purpose."* He also says: *"No weapon that is formed against thee shall prosper..."* His master plan tells us: *"For I know the plans I have for you,"* declares the LORD, *"plans to prosper you and not to harm you, plans to give you hope and a future."* Now, that is a master plan indeed!

III. GOD WILL MAKE YOU CONFIDENT BECAUSE OF HIS PRESENCE

God has made you conscious of your potential, He has commissioned you for a purpose, and in the final analysis, **you are confident because of His presence**. Judges 6:15-16 says: *"But Lord," Gideon asked, "how can I save Israel? My clan is the weakest in Manasseh, and I am the least in my family." The LORD answered, "I will be with you, and you will strike down all the Midianites together."*

Gideon says, "Lord, how am I going to do this? I am the least of the least; the last of the last." The angel says, "It is because God sponsors an affirmative action program." God has an affirmative action program that says: *"And now unto him who is able to do exceedingly abundantly, above all we can ask or think."* Do you have some stuff you didn't pray about and you never thought about, but God just blew your mind and did it for you anyway? That is God's affirmative action.

God's affirmative action means no devil in hell can block you, no hater can hinder you, and no racist can restrict you. God's affirmative action says, "whatever is for you, is for you, and nobody can stop what I have for you." God specializes in an affirmative action that says: *"The last shall be first."* That is what keeps me going especially when I look at the plight of black folk in this country. I know there is a God, and God has promised that *"the last shall be first."*

Once, after preaching for my best friend, Dr. Marvis May, in Baltimore, years ago, he took me to this high-class restaurant on the harbor. This was during the National Baptist Congress and it was packed out. In fact, we were last in line. So, here I am standing out the door; I can't get in because of the long line of folk in front of me. Marvis left me at the back of the line. He was gone for about five minutes, and I was beginning to wonder, "What's up?" Well, Marvis came back with the owner of the restaurant and the owner said to me, "I hear this is your best friend." I said, "Yes, he is." He said, "Well, your best friend is my best friend, and I would not let my best friend and his best friend stay in the back of this line. I have a suite where I eat that overlooks the restaurant. You all are going to be my guests, in my suite." I wish you could have seen me as I walked past everybody that was in front of me. I said, "What's up? I hope you enjoy your meal. Peace. God bless you!" I went from being last to being first; and not just first, I was in the suite looking down on folk.

If you feel you are the last of the last, just get with the One Who owns everything, and if you get with the One Who owns everything, and Who has the master plan, you will be cleared to take off and you will start flying at a higher level.

MY FAMILY IS A HOT MESS

Looking back on your family, would you characterize your family as a starting block or as a stumbling block? A starting block is designed to get you off to a good start. A stumbling block gets in your way and sometimes causes you to end up going down.

I repeat the question: was your family a good starting block because they helped get you off to a good start, or was your family a stumbling block because they tried to hinder you? Allow me to park here, and say, if God has blessed you with a strong family background, a praying mother or a praying big mama, somebody who took interest in you, thus providing you with a strong starting block, then that is something to thank God for. If you can look back in your life and note that where you are has a lot to do with the fact that God, in His grace and goodness, looked beyond your faults, saw your needs, and put the right people in your life, at just the right time, who were good starting blocks for you, then you ought to give God praise and be thankful.

On the other hand, there are some of us, if we are honest

with ourselves, who started out at a disadvantage because we did not have a family that was a good starting block; instead, they were a stumbling block. They were stumbling blocks because they told us we would never amount to anything. They were stumbling blocks, because, for whatever reason, they rejected us and made us feel as though we did not quite measure up to another sibling or measure up to somebody else. Worse than that, they mistreated us because of baby mama and baby daddy drama. Instead of loving and caring for us, oftentimes, a parent used us as a weapon or bargaining chip. Let me stop here and say, whenever you use your child as a weapon against your baby's daddy or your baby's mama, then that child will grow up and become a weapon. You can probably look back over your life and discover that maybe the reason you are where you are in the race of life is because you did not have a family that gave you a good starting block; instead, they were a stumbling block.

I came across a story that broke my heart. This particular family went on a camping trip during the heat of summer. As they were on this trip, the father, driving along with his wife and their two children made a wrong turn, and then things went dark. Shortly, after making that wrong turn, they discovered that they were on a loop, and consequently they kept going where they had already gone, doing what they had already done, seeing what they had already seen. To make matters worse, not only had it gotten dark, but a sudden storm hit; a flash flood came, literally blinding the view so that the daddy could not see in front of him. He accidentally ran up on something on the side of the road that blew two of his tires. Well, there they were—stuck. After the rain stopped, and with two tires blown, the father said, "Listen, it's dark out here. We don't know what animals are out there. So, I'm going to lock the doors and go search for help." The daddy left momma and his two kids in the car and went in search for help.

In the father's absence, the mother was physically beaten, the daughter was raped, and the son found himself handcuffed, helplessly held by those who were victimizing the daughter, the wife, and himself in the absence of the father. Understand how immensely angry the father was when he got back and found his family had been robbed, his wife beaten, his daughter raped, his son humiliated. When a reporter interviewed the father, he said, "All of this began when I made a wrong turn."

If we look back over our lives, can we be honest enough and admit, that maybe, things went wrong in our family because the person in charge made a wrong turn? Was it your father? Was it your mother? I don't know. But somebody made a wrong turn, and the sad thing is, you are still experiencing the consequences of the choice they made.

I'm going to hang out right here for a little while and exegete this illustration: there is a son who is now humiliated and grows up bitter, feeling insecure, and has an overwhelming sense of guilt because of what he witnessed but could do nothing about. Why? Because Daddy was gone and he had to witness a tragedy happen to his family. What about the poor daughter? The daughter finds herself violated and, of course, that is going to dictate how she interacts with other men in the future. Then there is the wife—battered and beaten. All of them find themselves on the victim end of a tragedy. Why? It all began when Daddy made a wrong turn.

Not only was there a wrong turn made, but they found themselves in a loop. Remember: I said earlier the daddy made a wrong turn and kept going where he had already been, seeing what he had already seen. They were caught up in a never-ending cycle—and a vicious cycle at that. Have you ever felt like you were a part of a vicious cycle, where you kept making the same mistakes; you kept seeing the same old reruns in your life?

I am dealing with this because as we look at our broken village, there are broken families in the broken village. Will you agree with me that the black family is in trouble? When it comes to every negative statistic, black families find themselves at the top of all of those troubling and negative statistics.

When we look at what's going on, we discover that we are in trouble because of what is happening with our black men. Many of our black fathers are either catching hell or raising hell. In many instances, our black fathers are stressed out and yet they remain strong. In other instances, we have fathers who have just given up and are absent. Other fathers are trying to do the right thing, but they are under attack, and the more they do right, the more evil is present with them. Some fathers are just doing what is wrong, and wrong keeps on following them.

Then, we have black mothers who also find themselves catching hell. After all, our sisters find themselves distressed and yet they are determined. They find themselves repressed, yet they are resilient. They find themselves stressed, yet they remain strong. How we thank God for our strong, resilient sisters, who refuse to give up! How we thank God for those mothers! Some of you can look at your own life and say, no, daddy wasn't around, but if it hadn't been for a praying mama who prayed me into church when I didn't have enough sense to go to church myself, where would I be?

Next, look at our poor children. Our children find themselves catching hell as well. They catch hell when they go to schools that are, in too many instances, inferior. We have teachers who cannot teach them and don't know how to deal with African-Americans and the different learning styles that our kids have. Our children are catching hell because, in too many instances, they live in homes where either the father is absent physically, or absent emotionally. (Fathers, just because you are there physically does not mean that you are there spiritually and emotionally.) On top of that, Mama is working so much that she hardly has time to give some love and share some presence, so the kids find themselves being raised either by the television or worse than that, on the internet where they are subjected to sexual perverts and individuals who prey on kids who are alone, abandoned, insecure, and vulnerable.

Our kids find themselves catching hell at home, at school, and in the streets. They are the product of a crack-culture, where their parents, in many instances, experimented with drugs, and now they find themselves with crack in their systems. Somewhere along the way, black folk made a wrong turn; we're caught up in a cycle and we are making our kids pay.

Now, let's turn to our text in Genesis 35:9-15, where we see that Jacob's family was also a hot mess. Not only was his immediate family a hot mess, but he came from a family that was a hot mess.

When Jacob was born, he was named Jacob by his parents. Jacob means: slick, conniving trickster. They named him that because when he came out of the womb he was clutching the heel of his brother, Esau. Understand, in biblical days, names were prophetic. They basically dictated the destiny of that child. Jacob finds himself in a family where his father favors his brother, Esau, and his mama favors him. Now, you know that is a hot mess right there! Can you imagine being a son in a male-dominated culture, and growing up in a household where you desire the affection of your daddy, but your daddy instead favors another sibling?

Your name may not be Jacob, but you know what it is like to grow up in a household, craving the affection, attention, and admiration of a parent, but their attention is someplace else, and you feel rejected by that parent. That is what was going on in Jacob's family. Even though he physically and geographically left that family and went to another area to find his own wife and begin his own family, that hot mess followed him.

If you don't deal with the family issues that you have in your blood stream, then you are going to carry the germs of your family's situation into your new family. I know some of you just couldn't wait to get married so that you could get out of mama's house. Well, if mama's house was a mess, and you came out of that mess, then guess what? If you are not careful, you can carry that mess into your new situation.

Let's take a look at Jacob's family mess: Jacob has two wives and two concubines, and twelve kids by these four different women. Think deeply about that—twelve kids by four different baby mamas, and the baby mamas don't like each other. Jacob really only loves one of them, but he has to put up with the rest of them, and he does because they all have children by him. And guess what? Because the baby mamas don't like each other, the kids don't like each other either. Now, that is a hot mess indeed!

The Bible says, Jacob has made so many wrong turns, he is caught up in a vicious cycle of dysfunctionality. Chapter thirty-four gives us a vivid description of Jacob's family mess. Because of Jacob's wrong turns, his daughter, Dinah, after going to visit the women of the land, was spotted by Shechem, the son of Hamor the Hivite, prince of the country, and Shechem raped her. After he physically violated her, Shechem decides he wants to marry her. Of course, Dinah's brothers are so upset that they concoct a scheme to get back at Shechem. Shechem falls in love with her, and they say, "okay, if you want to get married to our sister, all of the men in Shechem have to get circumcised." The Book says, while they are vulnerable because of where they have been cut, Jacob's sons now commit mass murder. They murder all the men in Shechem. So now, Jacob has a daughter who has been raped, he has sons who are gangsters, and he has wives who can't stand each other. What a hot mess!

All of us may not have a hot mess like that in our family, but we have some daddies who have strayed, we have some mamas who have been messed over, and we have some bad situations between sisters and brothers. Now, because this hot mess began when he made a wrong turn, Jacob is afraid that those who had been victimized are going to take out their revenge. Is a drive-by going to happen? Will his baby girl get shot?

Now, some of you may have moved into the suburbs and

thought you could get away from this problem, but it met you in the suburbs. You have gang activity in high school, middle school, and now they have begun to recruit, even in elementary school. Our kids are subject to gangs, guns, drugs, sexual perverts, and all kinds of negativity outside the home, and then they come home to a hot mess.

You may be wondering, is there any good news for somebody from a bad family? Yes, there is. Pastor John Claypool put it like this: "God is so amazingly good that only God can write straight on crooked lines." God can take the crooked lines of your life, and somehow write something straight on them. Many of you would not be where you are based on your family background. But, God said, "in spite of your family background, I'm going to write straight on your crooked lines."

There was another incident where another family found themselves lost, and this family also made a wrong turn, but they made use of OnStar. OnStar simply means you are a member of a network, and when you are a member of a network, the network always knows where you are. All you have to do is call up the network, and because the network is connected to a satellite above the earth, it knows exactly where you are. You can't see the satellite, but if you find yourself lost, all you have to do is call OnStar, and OnStar will give you directions from where you are to where you should be. You are all right today, because God hooked you up with the network. You can't see God. God is above everything. But the good news is, if you get with the network, God will set you free, God will speak to you, and God will order your steps to even overcome the hot mess of your family background.

You need to know, that even though your family is a hot mess right now, you can have a future that is God blessed. I love this because the text lets us know that God specializes in giving you the power to reinvent yourself by giving you a makeover. To get a makeover means you were one way, but then somehow you came out another way that was better than the way you were, to the point where folks don't even recognize you. Have you seen those shows where they give a makeover to a house? That means they go into a situation that is jacked-up, then they renovate that house, and by the time they get through renovating it, you see something that is brand new. Now, if they can do that on TV for a house, don't you know there is a God above Who specializes in going into messed up lives and giving complete makeovers? As the song by Howard E. Smith says:

> *I was sinking deep in sin,*
> *Far from the peaceful shore;*
> *Very deeply stained within,*
> *Sinking to rise no more.*
> *But the Master of the sea,*
> *Heard my despairing cry;*
> *From the waters He lifted me,*
> *Now safe am I.*

The Bible tells us in II Corinthians 5:17: *"Therefore if any man be in Christ, he is a new creature: old things are passed away; behold, all things are become new."*

The makeover begins when God allows you to come to the end of one chapter and He turns the page to begin the next chapter. All of Jacob's family mess took place in chapter thirty-four, which unfortunately ends on a bad note. It ends with Jacob's sons saying to him in response to Jacob asking them why had they killed those people: "you are just a wimp; we can't let them treat our sister like a prostitute."

It may seem like you're at the end of a chapter. Things may not be going well in your life. But, hold on; this just lets you know that you're at the end of a chapter, and a new chapter is about to begin.

Look at Genesis 35:1: *"Then God."* Because of those two words, I can stop right there and end this chapter. If these two words open up your next chapter, I promise you that your next chapter is going to be greater than your last chapter.

"Then God" means: God—Yahweh. God—Elohim. God—Jehovah-Jireh. God—Jehovah-Nissi. *"Then God"*—Jehovah-Shalom. *"Then God"*—Jehovah, My

Healer. *"Then God"*—Jehovah, My Shepherd. *"Then God"*—Emmanuel. *"Then God"*—Jehovah, My Provider.

"Then God"—heart fixer. *"Then God"*—mind regulator. *"Then God"*—burden bearer. *"Then God"*—heavy load sharer. *"Then God"*—rock in a weary land.

"Then God" showed up. That is all I need. I don't care how jacked-up my situation is, as long as God shows up! I don't care how badly I feel, as long as God shows up! I don't care how terrible things look, as long as God shows up!

I. GOD WILL CHANGE YOUR NAME

God showed up and said to Jacob, **"I'm going to change your name."** The Scripture says, *After Jacob returned from Paddan Aram, God appeared to him again and blessed him. God said to him, "Your name is Jacob, but you will no longer be called Jacob; your name will be Israel." So he named him Israel.* Now, like Jacob, you, too, are going from *used to be* to *going to be*.

All of us used to be something, but because God came into our situation, we went from used to be to going to be. God said, "what I'm going to do is change your name. I'm going to change what your parents put on you. Whatever your parents named you, that isn't going to be the name that is going to dictate the rest of your life." God is saying to you, "just because Daddy wasn't around, it doesn't mean that you can't be a good father. Just because your parents drank, it doesn't mean that you have to drink. Just because your parents were on crack, it doesn't mean you have to be on crack." God wants to break the cycle right now, and He wants to break the cycle beginning with you.

I know what Mama did, but the cycle is broken. I know stuff didn't work out between Mama and Daddy, but the cycle is broken. Maybe you were abused, but it doesn't mean you have to be an abuser, or allow yourself to be abused. The cycle is broken, and it starts with you, because once God changes you, then everybody else has to adjust to your change. No, I am not who I used to be. No, I don't go where I used to go. No, I won't let you talk to me like you used to talk to me, because I am not the same person you used to talk to, and so if you are going to come to me, you had better come correctly or don't come at all. It's a new day! And I'm a new person!

II. THOUGH THE WORST IS BEHIND YOU, THE BEST IS YET TO COME

The text also indicates, **though the worst is behind you, the best is yet to come.** The Scripture says: *And God said to him, "I am God Almighty; be fruitful and increase in number. A nation and a community of nations will come from you, and kings will come from your body. The land I gave to Abraham and Isaac I also give to you, and I will give this land to your descendants after you."* If you're not careful, you can allow what is behind you to confine you and define you, and it still affects you now.

In Exodus chapter three, you will discover that Moses' life is messed up. He is on the backside of the desert and God speaks to him through a bush that is burning, but isn't burning up. God says, "Moses, I'm going to use you to make a difference that is going to change this world." Moses says, "God, I do not have it like that." God says, "you have it because I'm going to use you to do it." Then Moses answers, "all right, but the folks are going to ask me what is Your name." And when Moses said that, God said, "Moses, what you want Me to do is define Myself, but if I define Myself, I'll confine Myself. See, one name isn't enough to really depict all that I am because sometimes I make a way out of no way. Other times, I heal. Other times, I open doors. Other times, I provide. Other times, I give you peace. If I just give you one name, that is going to put some limitations on Me. So, when the folks ask you to say My name, just tell them, *I Am*. Because that is all you need. Whatever you need, *I Am*. If you're hungry, I am bread. If you're thirsty, I am water. If you're locked in, I am the way out. If you're confused, I am your 'peace that passeth all understanding.'"

To Jacob He said, *"I am God Almighty."* The Hebrew word there is *El Shaddai*. If you want healing from family dysfunction, the healing begins when God puts a change in you, and when you have so much confidence in Who God is, that you are now conscious of Whose you are, and you are comforted in knowing what you will do.

God said, "I am El Shaddai." This word first appears in Genesis seventeen, when the Bible says that Abraham and Sarah laughed at God when He said, "Abraham, as old as you all are, you are going to have a child." Sarah cracked up. She was thinking, "there is no way we are going to have a child. In the first place, Viagra has not been invented, and in the second place, there is no Cialis around. To make matters worse, I'm post-menopausal. I do not have any children, and I am not going to have any children." My Bible tells me that God overheard Sarah laughing and said, "all right I'm going to show you who gets the last laugh." And the Bible says, God said, "My name is El Shaddai." What does El Shaddai mean? It means the Almighty, Omnipotent God Who is Self-Sustaining and specializes in bringing possibilities out of impossibilities. By the way, Abraham and Sarah did have a son. His name was Isaac.

So when God appeared to Jacob, He said: "I am El Shaddai; I'm Omnipotent; I'm Almighty; I specialize in bringing new possibilities out of terrible impossibilities; I specialize in new beginnings out of old messed up situations." And that is what God is saying to you right now: "I don't care how old and messed up your situation has been. I specialize in bringing new possibilities into a bad situation." Isn't that some good news? Regardless of how bad your family background may be, God specializes in making all things new. God will do a brand new thing. He will change your life, He will change your situation, and He will change you.

III. COMMEMORATE WHAT YOU ANTICIPATE

In the final analysis, make sure you **commemorate what you anticipate**. The Scripture says: *"Jacob set up a stone pillar at the place where God had talked with him, and he poured out a drink offering on it; he also poured oil on it. Jacob called the place where God had talked with him Bethel."* Commemorate what you anticipate.

I'll never forget when I went to Africa for the first time; I went to Abidjan, and they took us to this sister's house. On the wall of this sister's home is a mural. It didn't have a frame. Of course, we asked how that happened.

She said, "I was having a party here when I first moved in, and one of my neighbors splashed some grape soda on the wall which left a stain that I could not get out. I was upset because it was a beautiful white wall. No matter what I tried, I just could not get the grape stain out. So my father says, 'Listen, baby, I'll take care of this.' And I said, 'But, Daddy, what am I going to do?' He said, 'Don't you worry, I'm going to take care of it. I've always come through for you, and I'll come through now.'"

Her daddy had her move out of the house for a week, and while she was gone, he hired an artist who was a friend of his. This artist is one of the best known artists on the West Coast of Africa. The artist painted a mural using the grape stain as background, and now the value of the house has escalated in such a marvelous fashion: first, because of the fact that there is a mural where there had just been white walls, and then, second, because of whose name is signed on the painting that is on the wall. What was a mess is now a masterpiece. This is what she said, "I trusted my Daddy, and left my house, and while I was away, my Daddy hired somebody to convert my mess into a masterpiece."

Well, if her earthly father did that for her, can you imagine what a masterpiece your Heavenly Father will produce out of your family mess?

Jacob commemorates what he anticipates. The text says, he names the place Bethel which means "house of God." Jacob recognizes his family has been a hot mess, and now he renames his mess the House of God. If you want your family to go from a hot mess to a house of God, I dare you to rename your household, and say from now on, this is God's house, this is God's kitchen, this is God's bedroom, this is God's living room—this is the house of God! Even though your family may be a hot mess, your future is God blessed.

You Were Born to Blow Up

"And he named his second son Ephraim, because God has made me fruitful in the land of my suffering."
—Genesis 41:52

Would it not be downright ridiculous if you came to the plate in a baseball game every time it was your turn at bat and you already had two strikes against you? Would it not be downright unjust if you were playing basketball, and your opponent was privileged to play with regulation size goals that were ten feet high, but you had to play with goals that were twenty feet high—same court, but different goals? Would it not be ridiculously unjust if you were playing football against your opponent, and you discover that they had to go one hundred yards to score a touchdown, but whenever your team had the ball, the length of the field was extended another fifty yards?

All of these are ridiculous propositions, but I think you recognize the analogy, and that is, sadly, we still live in a nation where we are judged by the color of our skin and not "the content of our character." Mama was on it when she declared, you still have to work twice as hard to get half as much, and be twice as good to be accepted.

I shall never forget reading about Clare Boothe Luce. Clare Boothe Luce was an ambassador to Italy, and while serving her ambassadorship, she had a villa where she lived. At one point, she became gravely ill and the doctors could not understand why. They later discovered that she was poisoned. There were toxins in her system, and so they began to check the food by having other people eat the same food that she was eating. The food was okay, and so they kept on checking until one day, they discovered that there were tiny particles falling from the ceiling. The tiny particles turned out to be lead, and those lead particles were creating a toxic environment for Clare Boothe Luce.

Clare found herself living in a place that was taking the life out of her. She was in an atmosphere that was adversarial. I don't know about you, but recently, I've been fascinated by the series of articles in *U.S.A. Today* regarding the fact that where you live determines how long you live. In other words, what determines economic opportunity as well as quality of healthcare in a given area is your zip code. None of us are surprised that the majority of the areas where there is a high infant mortality rate and where there is a limited life expectancy happens to be areas that are occupied by persons whose skin has been darkened by nature's sun.

To some of you young people who have graduated or who are just graduating from college, I am glad that God has blessed you to survive, but please recognize that you are moving into a world that is unjust and unfair. You are moving into a world that sadly, sinfully, and shamefully will still judge you by what they see on the surface, before they get to know the substance of your spirit and character, and who you really are. Now, that may be the world's issue, but it doesn't have to be your issue. Why? Because God has major love for you. He did not make you by accident. God brought you to this planet by divine arrangement. You have an appointment to keep with the destiny that God has divinely designed for you. Yes, I know there is a world of racial injustice out there. Yes, sadly, they still redline our community and this precludes us from economic development.

I read a report that stated that on average, when African-Americans go to buy a car, they pay at least 3% more, in terms of interest, than white Americans. You are going into a world where the football field is longer for you to score a touchdown than for others, but again don't let that get to you because you serve a God Who specializes in fighting for those who are disadvantaged and somehow turns their disadvantages into advantages.

You may have experienced those who have tried to hold you down and keep you back, but everything they did to keep you back only set you up for what God had in store for you. And that is my word to you today: *you were born to blow up.*

How do I know? In our text, Joseph was in the land of his suffering—Egypt. Joseph's wife, Asenath, who was an Egyptian beauty, had just given birth to their two children. Joseph said, "I'm naming my firstborn, Manasseh, because God has let me forget all the hell my family put me through." Please understand, if you don't check your baggage, your baggage will wreck you. I don't care what other folk have done to you, please don't give them the final victory over you, to the point where you are moving into your future still carrying baggage that they placed in your life.

Joseph names his second child, Ephraim. Ephraim means "fruitful." Some translators say it means "double prosperity." Joseph insightfully interprets Ephraim to mean God has made me fruitful in the land of my suffering. Joseph said, "in the very land where I caught nothing but hell, God has made me fruitful. In the very land that has been adversarial to my existence, God has made me fruitful." You must recognize that in spite of being in an atmosphere that may be against you, God has put something in you that nobody can stop, and consequently, you can say, God has made me fruitful in the land of my suffering.

The text also lets us know that Joseph did good, but received bad in return. Doesn't it blow your mind how that sometimes, no matter how much good you try to do, evil always shows up? And no matter how much you do the right thing, wrong comes your way? Unfortunately, this happens in life.

The Bible tells us what happened to Joseph in chapter thirty-nine of Genesis. Joseph was sold into slavery by his own brothers, and while he was in slavery he worked hard because he was not going to allow the situation he was in to get in him and take out of him what God had placed in him. So, he worked with a 5-star mentality, even while a slave in Potiphar's house. The Book says that Potiphar saw that God was blessing him and Joseph got promoted; he was the number one servant in Potiphar's household. The Bible says, once he blew up, Sister Potiphar began to notice him. The text points out that Joseph was built and handsome, but Potiphar's wife didn't notice he was handsome until he blew up.

Some people are not going to think about you until they see you begin to blow up. You have to watch people like that, because anybody who wants to get with you for what you can do and not for who you are, isn't worthy of you. If they ask you what do you do, say, "what I do is none of your business, but if you check out who I am I may bless you with what I do."

Sister Potiphar chooses to step toward Joseph, but then Joseph tells her, I am not going out like that. In the words of singer, Beyonce, "You must not know 'bout me. To the left. To the left." Sister Potiphar lies and screams rape, and when she screams rape, Joseph gets sent to prison without due process. There is no Johnny Cochran to get him off.

There is no Project Innocence to exonerate him with DNA evidence. Joseph gets thrown into prison for something he did not do. I want you to know there is a lot of injustice out there, especially in the criminal "injustice" system. Joseph is thrown into prison for something he did not do, and then while he is in prison, he is forgotten by somebody he did something good for. Doesn't it trip you out that as long as folk need you, you can find them, but the moment you need them, they suddenly vanish?

The Bible says that Joseph interprets the dream of the chief butler, and when the butler is set free, Joseph tells the butler, "when you get up to the big house, don't forget about me. Don't go Clarence Thomas on me, and forget where you came from, but help me get out of this place." But, once the butler gets up there, he goes Clarence Thomas; he suddenly gets amnesia. He is back in the big house, and has forgotten about the Joseph who helped him get back to the big house. Joseph is now languishing in a waiting room of helplessness, and there is nothing he can do to get his situation resolved.

Let me hang out right here for a while because I think all of us have been there—in a waiting room, hoping and praying that something will happen, but nothing happens. We've done all we could do. We've stood as much as we could stand, but guess what? In spite of all of that standing, years have gone by and it seems like God has turned a deaf ear to our pleas and our prayers. Now, you can play holy on me all you want to, but God doesn't always move when we want Him to move. As a matter of fact, if I were God, I would have blessed me a long time ago. But God takes His time.

The Bible says that while Joseph was languishing in prison, God had Pharaoh to dream a dream that Pharaoh could not interpret. Joseph is in prison wondering where God is, and while Joseph is wondering where God is, God is working out His plan, without Joseph's knowledge. That is how good God is. God is so good that while you're over here waiting for God to speak, God will be doing something, somewhere else. Why? Because God always knows when to touch the right person at the right time who will do the right thing, in order for you to receive what God has in store for you.

Notice that Joseph's gift was manifested while he was suffering. It was while Joseph was in prison that Joseph interpreted the dream of the baker and the butler. You never really find out all that God has put in you until you go through some things. You never really find yourself until you go through some stuff that you never thought you would have to go through. God has a way of using what comes up against us to bring something out of us that we never knew we had in us.

Wait, it's about to get better. Joseph hears the good news that Pharaoh can't interpret his own dream. The text goes on to say that Joseph is set free; he interprets Pharaoh's dream, and then Joseph is given a position where he enacts public policy for future possibility. Joseph engages in his new position with what I call **policies of possibilities.** Joseph gets selected for office as Prime Minister of Agriculture and Commerce and Joseph's first policy is a *policy of possibility.*

How I wish that we had an administration in Washington, D.C. that would enact *policies of possibilities.* Instead, it has been an administration that has enacted policies that have aborted possibilities. Our national debt is a disgrace. How do you inherit a surplus from the prior administration, and yet end up in debt to China and other nations? It's because of the stewardship, the sinful stewardship of greed in the White House, that has cut taxes for the wealthy, while at the same time has cut funding to programs of possibility. How can you cut programs of possibility like Head-start? How can you cut programs of possibility like Upward Bound? How can you cut programs of possibility, and then fund an unjust, uncalled for, unethical war over in Iraq? There are no policies of possibilities, but policies that abort possibilities. May God give our governmental leaders the wisdom to enact policies of possibilities in education; policies of possibilities to face down poverty and eradicate poverty; policies of possibilities in our poorest communities—may we have a brand new day of policies of possibilities. That is what Joseph did.

But I am not really dealing with Joseph, I'm dealing with the Ephraim generation, because that is who you are. You represent the Ephraim generation. You represent the descendants of Joseph. You weren't the slaves; Joseph was. You didn't go through the civil rights struggle; Joseph did. And since you didn't go through all of that, that means you are heirs to a legacy of power, liberation, and dignity. God says that you are the Ephraim generation. **You were born to blow up.**

You may be thinking, "Pastor Haynes, my name is not Ephraim." Correct. But your name is what your name is. And you will give meaning to your name by the life that you lead. Martin Luther King, Jr. gave meaning to his name. Frederick Douglass gave meaning to his name.

Speaking of Frederick Douglass, I was told this story while I was growing up, and it blessed and changed my life. There was this little boy growing up in West Virginia and at the age of four, both his parents died. Broke and poor, he was raised by his sister. This boy went to school and when they asked him what his name was, he had to make up a name because he did not know his real name. Well, he had been told a lot about the silver-tongued orator of the abolitionist movement, Frederick Douglass, and he said, "well, my name is Frederick Douglass." That is the name that he took. His teacher, upon learning that he had taken that name for himself said, "That is quite a name. Now, make sure that you live up to that name."

He said he spent the rest of his life trying to live up to the name that he had taken for himself. What did he do? He finished high school, and then worked his way across the United States, from West Virginia to Los Angeles, California, setting up pins in bowling alleys because they did not have the automatic setup back then. Once he got to Los Angeles, he received his undergraduate degree from the University of Southern California and went to Biola University. He kept on working because he had a name that he was living up to. He was called to pastor Second Baptist Church in Fresno, California, where he organized the first youth church in that state. He was then called to pastor Third Baptist Church in San Francisco. He did something else in San Francisco—he was the first African-American ever to run for the county board of supervisors in San Francisco, which opened up the door for other African-Americans to be elected to office in San Francisco. He had a name he was living up to. In 1948, he addressed the Democratic National Convention, and he kept on living up to that name.

How do I know so much about this person? I know so much because he is my grandfather, Frederick Douglass Haynes, Sr., who named his son, Frederick Douglass Haynes, Jr., who named his son, Frederick Douglass Haynes, III. Do you want to know why I do what I do? It is because I have a name to live up to. Guess what? You have a name to live up to, as well. You don't know that name? Well, ask Jesus what your name is, and He will tell you: Royal Priesthood—live up to it! What is your name? Child of God—live up to it! What is your name? Chosen Generation—live up to it!

So, you ask, how do I live up to my name? Let me give you three ways you can live up to your name:

I. BE CONSCIOUS OF YOUR HISTORY

You have to be conscious of your history. In the text, Joseph named his second child, Ephraim—because Joseph said the Lord made me "fruitful in the land of my suffering." Joseph gave his child an identity to live up to. Fathers, whatever else we do, we must realize that God has given us the power as the paternal parent to shape the identity of our children.

Joseph named his son Ephraim, and said you need to have a sense of history. Every time your name is called, remember where you came from, because if you don't know where you came from, you are not going to get to where you are trying to go. So Joseph said, "remember, overcoming is in your DNA, because if the enemies of your ancestors had their way, you wouldn't even be born."

The very fact that you are black and living in this country is evidence of the power of God to work miracles in the face of oppression, and it is also evidence of the strength of our ancestors who survived the heinous horrors of the Middle Passage.

How do you survive being kept on a ship like sardines, and then treated, not as a person to be respected, but as a piece of property? How do you survive slavery? How do you survive second-class citizenship? That is what it means to be a descendant of Joseph—you are a survivor. If our ancestors could survive slavery and if they could survive second-class citizenship, I know we can survive whatever may come our way. As you become aware of your history, you will learn how to hold on when God has you on hold, because you trust that God is holding what He has uniquely designed for you. Do you know why God has you on hold? God has you on hold because He is holding what He has for you so that nobody can take it from you.

Recently, I went to Neiman Marcus and while I was browsing the store, I came across a rack of clothes, and I saw something that I really liked. I went to that rack to pull it down, but the sign on the top of the rack said "hold", and all of the outfits on that rack had names on them. I knew what "hold" meant, but playing dumb, I said to the man who was helping me, "Man, check this. This is the outfit I've been looking for. Plus, it's my size. Can I have this?" The man said, "Pastor, I know you can read. That sign says 'hold.'" I replied, "But it's in your store for sale." He said, "Yeah, but not to you." He said, "Pastor, I love and respect you, but you have to understand something, when it says 'hold' and there is a name attached to it, that means it belongs to that person, and we are not supposed to let anybody come in here and take it because it is on hold for that person."

God says, whatever I have for you, don't you worry about it. It may take you some time to get to where you are trying to go, but God has some blessings with your name on them. God has some blessings on hold for you.

II. CLAIM YOUR IDENTITY

After you are conscious of your history, **then you can claim your identity**. Joseph said to his son, Ephraim, your name means "fruitful." I don't care where you are or what you are going through, remember who you are. If you are in a famine, your name is fruitful. If you are catching hell, your name is fruitful. If folks steal from you and try to block your blessings, your name is fruitful. Regardless of where you are and what may happen to you, don't you ever forget who you are.

That is my word to you: don't you ever forget who you are, because God is so amazingly, wonderfully good that He has given you a sense of identity, and who you are is never determined by where you are. As a matter of fact, who you are can reshape wherever you are, if you remain true to who you are. You are not a thermometer, you are a thermostat. A thermometer registers the temperature; a thermostat regulates the temperature. A thermometer is controlled by the atmosphere; a thermostat controls the atmosphere. When you know who you are, you can regulate wherever you are.

III. CLAIM YOUR DATE WITH DESTINY

Finally, **claim your date with destiny**. Now, in the Afro-

Asiatic culture in which Joseph was living, the parents didn't give names to their children that sounded cute. The names always meant something because the names gave a clue to the children's character, or better still, it was a prophecy of what that child would become. When Jesus was born, what did the angel say to Joseph? He said, you are going to name Him Jesus. What does Jesus mean? It means "God Saves" or "Yahweh Saves" because, **"He is going to save His people from their sins."** His name was a prophecy of what He was going to become. And guess what? Your name is Ephraim. You may not be fruitful right now, but if you keep on living, your name is a prophecy of what you shall become. So, go ahead, claim your possibility, and claim your date with destiny.

I saw this movie I thought I would never watch because it did not appeal to me. But this movie arrested my attention on TV, late one night. The name of the movie is *Simon Birch. Simon Birch* is based on the novel about the life of Owen Meany. Simon Birch was born in a deformed fashion. He was tiny and had an enormously small heart.

The doctor in the movie said that Simon was not going to live more than twenty-four hours after his birth. (Let me hasten to say, that as much as I respect the medical profession, don't you ever allow anybody to be God in your life except God.) Contrary to what the doctor said, Simon Birch lived well into his teenage years. While growing up, everybody looked down on him, and even his own parents were disappointed that they had a child who was abnormal and tiny. Consequently, Simon Birch caught hell at home; he went to school and was teased; he even went to his preacher, and his low-down preacher didn't even believe when Simon said, "God has made me for a purpose. I believe in spite of my small size that God is going to use me and I'm going to be somebody special. As a matter of fact, I'm going to be somebody's hero."

Imagine having that kind of audacity: your parents don't believe in you, your preacher looks down on you, the doctor says you are not supposed to be here, your friends are teasing you, and yet you have the audacity to believe **you were born to blow up**. Well, that is Simon Birch. One day, as an adolescent, his class went on a bus trip. The bus driver swerved to avoid hitting something, and when he swerved, the bus flipped over. When the bus flipped over, Simon Birch and the other kids were in a bad way. But do you know what happened? Simon Birch, with his little self, found a window that had been jarred loose by the crash, and Simon, taking charge, told the other kids, "come here, come through this window right here." The same kids who had been dogging him are now following him. You see, if you stay with God long enough, God will flip the script. God will turn the tables.

Simon said, "You all come here," and one by one, the children got through the window, and after Simon got all of them out, he got himself out. But Simon was severely injured, and ended up in the hospital. His best friend, who did not believe in God, was trying to comfort him.

Simon said to his friend, "I did good, didn't I?" His friend replied, "Yes, you did." Simon said, "I told you I would amount to something. As a matter of fact, that window was just my size. That is how you all got set free." Soon after, Simon died, but he knew that his life meant something, because his best friend, who did not believe in God, now believes in God because of Simon's heroism.

Simon blew up because he kept on believing when nobody else would believe. I hope you will say, "you know what, I'm going to believe, regardless of what may come. If my friends talk about me, if other folks dog me, I'm going to believe because I was **born to blow up.**"

"If God be for you, who can be against you?" Blow up! *"Greater is He that is in you, than he that is in the world."* Blow up! *"I can do all things through Christ who strengthens me."* Blow up! *"The Lord is my light and my salvation, whom shall I fear."* Blow up! Blow up! Blow up! And when you get to the top and people ask you how did you get there, just tell them, "I was **born to blow up.**"

Sexual Healing

In those days Israel had no king. Now a Levite who lived in a remote area in the hill country of Ephraim took a concubine from Bethlehem in Judah. But she was unfaithful to him. She left him and went back to her father's house in Bethlehem, Judah. After she had been there four months, her husband went to her to persuade her to return. He had with him his servant and two donkeys. She took him into her father's house, and when her father saw him, he gladly welcomed him. His father-in-law, the girl's father, prevailed upon him to stay; so he remained with him three days, eating and drinking, and sleeping there.

On the fourth day they got up early and he prepared to leave, but the girl's father said to his son-in-law, "Refresh yourself with something to eat; then you can go." So the two of them sat down to eat and drink together. Afterward the girl's father said, "Please stay tonight and enjoy yourself." And when the man got up to go, his father-in-law persuaded him, so he stayed there that night. On the morning of the fifth day, when he rose to go, the girl's father said, "Refresh yourself. Wait till afternoon!" So the two of them ate together.

73

Then when the man, with his concubine and his servant, got up to leave, his father-in-law, the girl's father, said, "Now look, it's almost evening. Spend the night here; the day is nearly over. Stay and enjoy yourself. Early tomorrow morning you can get up and be on your way home." But, unwilling to stay another night, the man left and went toward Jebus (that is, Jerusalem), with his two saddled donkeys and his concubine.

When they were near Jebus and the day was almost gone, the servant said to his master, "Come, let's stop at this city of the Jebusites and spend the night."

His master replied, "No. We won't go into an alien city, whose people are not Israelites. We will go on to Gibeah." He added, "Come, let's try to reach Gibeah or Ramah and spend the night in one of those places." So they went on, and the sun set as they neared Gibeah in Benjamin. There they stopped to spend the night. They went and sat in the city square, but no one took them into his home for the night.

That evening an old man from the hill country of Ephraim, who was living in Gibeah (the men of the place were Benjamites), came in from his work in the fields. When he looked and saw the traveler in the city square, the old man asked, "Where are you going? Where did you come from?"

He answered, "We are on our way from Bethlehem in Judah to a remote area in the hill country of Ephraim where I live. I have been to Bethlehem in Judah and now I am going to the house of the LORD. No one has taken me into his house. We have both straw and fodder for our donkeys and bread and wine for ourselves your servants—me, your maidservant, and the young man with us. We don't need anything."

"You are welcome at my house," the old man said. "Let me supply whatever you need. Only don't spend the night in the square." So he took him into his house and fed his donkeys. After they had washed their feet, they had something to eat and drink.

While they were enjoying themselves, some of the wicked men of the city surrounded the house. Pounding on the door, they shouted to the old man who owned the house, "Bring out the man who came to your house so we can have sex with him."

The owner of the house went outside and said to them, "No, my friends, don't be so vile. Since this man is my guest, don't do this disgraceful thing. Look, here is my virgin daughter, and his concubine. I will bring them out to you now, and you can use them and do to them whatever you wish. But to this man, don't do such a disgraceful thing."

But the men would not listen to him. So the man took his concubine and sent her outside to them, and they raped her and abused her throughout the night, and at dawn they let her go. At daybreak the woman went back to the house where her master was staying, fell down at the door and lay there until daylight.

When her master got up in the morning and opened the door of the house and stepped out to continue on his way, there lay his concubine, fallen in the doorway of the house, with her hands on the threshold. He said to

her, "Get up; let's go." But there was no answer. Then the
man put her on his donkey and set out for home.
    When he reached home, he took a knife and cut
up his concubine, limb by limb, into twelve parts and
sent them into all the areas of Israel. Everyone who saw
it said, "Such a thing has never been seen or done, not
since the day the Israelites came up out of Egypt. Think
about it! Consider it! Tell us what to do!"

—Judges 19

Whenever you have been wounded psychologically, it sets
the stage for you to do some warped things biologically.
In other words, whenever you have been scarred
emotionally, it sets the stage for you to look for ways to
medicate your misery, and oftentimes, we medicate our
misery by doing that which is warped, biologically. Allow
me to raise three questions: Have you ever been wounded
emotionally? Have you ever had something to happen to
you that left you wondering, will I ever be able to get up?
Do you look for ways to medicate your misery? In too
many instances, we seek something physical to remedy
that which is emotional, psychological, or spiritual.

Allow me to raise another question: What is it that has
really messed you up? It may have happened way back,
and yet, it still messes with you even today. In other words,
there is some pain in your past that has become an invisible
puppeteer. You've seen puppets. Puppets are controlled
by puppeteers that pull their strings. To the naked eye, it
appears that the puppet is moving on its own, but actually

there is something off-stage that is pulling the strings and causing the puppet to move in this direction or that direction. Many of us will admit that we have a puppeteer from our past that somehow pulls our strings, and we find ourselves incarcerated with certain internal issues, such as insecurity, low self-esteem, and fear. For some of us, even though we were hurt back then, we can still feel the wounds even today. And if we are not careful, we may look for physical ways to medicate what is a spiritual, emotional, or psychological pain. If you don't believe that, let's check out the life of Marvin Gaye.

Marvin Gaye, that crooner with soul; Marvin Gaye, the mentor to Stevie Wonder; Marvin Gaye, the pied piper of Motown, threw down and had it going on. Marvin Gaye was the precursor to the Luther Vandrosses of our day, in that he brought eroticism to the wax. He brought eroticism to the wax in how he sang with eloquence about sex. He sang, "Got to give it up," and "Let's get it on." Marvin Gaye blatantly and brilliantly utilized sex to share his message. But, when you study the life of Marvin Gaye, you will discover that he grew up in a rigid, religious, restricted household where his father, Rev. Gaye, was a strict preacher, and consequently, there were strict rules that he had to adhere to, which sometimes manifested itself in the physical abuse of Marvin and his siblings.

According to Dr. Michael Eric Dyson, in his classic work about Marvin Gaye, Marvin Gaye was allegedly raped at the age of fifteen, by his own uncle. Marvin Gaye was in the bathroom. His uncle knocked on the door, stating that he needed to use the restroom, and while Marvin rushed to finish, his uncle burst through the door, and said, "I want you to stay right here as I use the restroom." Marvin said, "That is no thing to do for a real man." His uncle said, "You better stay in here." He threatened fifteen year old Marvin, and as he began to use the restroom, he then had Marvin handle him and in handling him, Marvin was upset and the more he got upset, the more his uncle threatened him by saying, "I heard your daddy beat you last night. Imagine if I tell him what a bad kid you are. You think last night was bad; tonight will be even worse." Then he bent Marvin over the sink, and violently and brutally raped him.

Imagine how Marvin must have felt as he was now incarcerated by insecurity. Why? Because now at the age of fifteen (and you do recognize that at this age, teenagers are in a twilight zone of searching for their identities), Marvin Gaye was brutally violated by someone he thought he could trust, someone he thought cared about him and loved him. Now, he is questioning his own sexuality.

On the stage, Marvin was quite a star; publicly he was a major success; but privately, his life was a hot mess. No wonder Marvin got caught up in the drug world. No wonder he had one broken relationship after another.

While he was in Europe, one of his acquaintances realized that he was throwing his life away on drugs, and said to him, "What you need is some sexual healing." That gave rise to the song that became so popular—"Sexual Healing." When you looked at him externally, it appeared that all was well, but internally, he was severely wounded.

May I stop right there and make a suggestion: maybe you ought not to judge people based on what you see on the outside, because you never know what wounds they are carrying on the inside. Marvin Gaye blew up as a star, but he was low emotionally because of his scars. And that is where you might be right now. You know what it's like to find yourself violated by someone you thought you could trust; you know what it is like to wrestle with yourself about your own insecurity about who you are because of some things that were done to you that you had no control over.

I am going to spend some time here because our community is still suffering from the vestiges of slavery. We are the product of post-traumatic slavery syndrome, in that, as a people, we still have not had the time to sit down and work therapeutically through all of the issues of four hundred years of brutal slavery, four hundred years of oppression, four hundred years of being treated not as persons to be respected, but as things to be used.

One area in which we especially have that revelation and manifestation is in the area of our sexuality. Why? Because during slavery, our men were emasculated and our sisters were treated as sexual objects—they had no control over their bodies. Men had to watch their women being brutally raped by the master. Can you imagine what that did to a brother, as he watched his own woman, that he loved, brutally taken and raped? He had no say, whatsoever, over her body, and consequently, he was emotionally and psychologically emasculated about his own manhood. Whenever you have been emasculated, you may engage in overcompensation and maybe that is what many brothers are guilty of. And, in spite of our having survived and come through slavery, we are still overcompensating from the emasculating experience of slavery.

What do I mean? Why is it, in the mindset of a brother, that he equates his manhood with the number of women he has, as opposed to his ability to be committed to loving one woman as Jesus Christ loved the church? Let me tell you something, brother, having a whole lot of kids by different women doesn't make you a man—dogs do that. It takes a man to raise a child. It takes a man to lovingly be loyal to a woman. We have allowed post-traumatic slavery syndrome to make us overcompensate.

Then, our sisters find themselves sexually objectified. Notice, if you will, our sisters often overcompensate— they go to one of two extremes. Some sisters are downright frigid, and they are so cold sexually, that there seems to be a wall around them. Then there are other sisters who are downright "hoochified," in terms of their sexual exploits, and they move from bed to bed to bed.

At one of our local high schools in Texas, we are told of the many different manifestations of sexual dysfunction that are going on with the teenagers, and this is not just in high school, but in middle school and in elementary school as well. We have girls who are now experimenting with other girls. And then we have girls who find themselves giving boys oral sex and convincing themselves that they have not engaged in sex because they are giving oral sex. Then we have a new breed of relationships; they call it "friends with benefits"—there is no commitment. They say, "we'll just have sex, but there is no commitment, there is no companionship. We'll just make each other feel good."

This sexual dysfunction is a reflection of the brokenness in our community. One cannot watch a rap video without seeing our sisters being exploited. There is a need for healing in our community.

Our text relates to us a sad and sick story. Bible readers recognize that the book of Judges is one vicious cycle of the people of God turning from God and then being oppressed as they are punished by God; then they turn back to God and are delivered by God. Then the cycle repeats itself. It's a nasty, vicious cycle of the same old thing—they kept doing what they were doing and kept getting what they were getting.

I pause to ask you, could that be your story when it comes

to sexual dysfunction—you're doing what you've been doing, and getting what you've been getting? And here's the thing that is so mind-blowing—A whole lot of folk go to church, turn to God, then they leave church and turn back to their old ways. Then they find themselves in a jacked-up situation because every time you lay down with dogs you come up with fleas. Then they seek God again to deliver them, and the cycle starts all over again.

I want to unpack this hot mess in Judges, and talk about three things: (1) there is a sickness that handicaps us, (2) there are symptoms that hurt us, and then (3) there are solutions that will heal us.

I. THE SICKNESS THAT HANDICAPS US

We must realize that there is a **sickness that handicaps us**. Judges 19:1 says: *In those days Israel had no king. Now a Levite who lived in a remote area in the hill country of Ephraim took a concubine from Bethlehem in Judah.* The Bible says, in terms of the sickness that handicaps us, that there is perversion and profanity that brings pain. I'll break it down for you: notice that the whole thing begins because there is a praise member—a Levite—one who is set aside to offer praises to God, who hooks up with a woman, but never upgrades her to the status of wife.

The Levite hooks up with a concubine. A concubine is a second-class wife. (That is a nice way of putting it.) A concubine was really just a slave for the purpose of sex. A concubine was one who would be there when the man said, "whenever my appetite is ready, you are supposed to be there to do what I need done, so I can have my appetite satisfied." Sisters, from this concubine you can learn that whenever you begin on a concubine level, don't get upset if you never get upgraded to wife status. In most cases, if you begin concubine, you stay concubine.

Recently, on the NBC Today Show, they were talking about the fact that a whole lot of fires that have been started in homes, began in the bed. So I checked out one story about this woman who barely escaped with her life. Her body was covered with about 80% burns from a fire that started in her home. She said that the fire began because she was smoking in bed, she had newspapers all around her, plus she had other papers she was grading. A whole lot of activity was going on in her bed. Anyway, while smoking in bed, she dozed off. The bed sheets caught on fire along with the newspapers and the papers she was grading. When the reporters asked this woman what happened, she replied, "I almost lost my life. I did lose my house because I had too much going on in my bed." There are some sisters whose lives are broken right now because they just have too much going on in their bed. When you have too much going on in your bed, you set yourself up to be destroyed.

The text says she was a concubine, but what is shocking is that it was her daddy who allowed this activity. A lot of sisters begin and stay at "hoochified" status because of the negative signals they received from their fathers. It is that relationship with your father that sent you signals, because the first man you were ever supposed to fall in love with was your father. If your father's relationship with you was dysfunctional, or if your father's relationship with you was healthy, that sent a signal that you internalized whether positive or negative. The signals that you internalized, you took with you into the world, and as you moved out into the world, you sent out those signals. Do you want to know why it is that you keep drawing the same kind of men into your life? It is because there is a signal that has been given to you and you, in return, are giving off that same signal. That is why I often say, "quit calling every man a dog." All men are not dogs. It's just that every man you hook up with happens to be a dog. So since you are the common denominator, and all your men are dogs, you need to stop serving up "Kibbles and Bits." This woman's father set her up for this kind of "hoochified" existence.

But, not only that: the text further tells us that after a while, (and there is some controversy as to what the actual translation is; one translation says that she had an affair and that is why she left; the majority of translations, say that she had a quarrel with her husband) and without notice, she reached a point in her life where her boundaries said, I'm not going to put up with this anymore. I'm not going to allow you to disrespect me anymore.

Judges 19:2 says: ***But she was unfaithful to him. She left him and went back to her father's house in Bethlehem, Judah.*** She pulled a Popeye and basically said, I've had all I can stand. (When did Popeye reach that point? When Brutus was beating him down, and he beat him down so much, that something came into Popeye that put some power back in him.) I hope some sister, after reading this, will look at any situation that is beneath her dignity, and beneath her self-respect, and say, I've had all I can stand and I can't stand it anymore.

The text goes on to say that she went home to her father, and after four months had passed, all of a sudden, what was in her past came to get her. Judges 19:3 says: ***Her husband went to her to persuade her to return. He had with him his servant and two donkeys. She took him into her father's house, and when her father saw him, he gladly welcomed him.*** I have to be real with you, because a lot of us are in church and we are all excited because the Lord changed our lives and we think, the Lord has saved me, the Lord has changed me, and everything is just fine. But, if you are not careful, it's the stuff that is in your past that can come up to haunt you, handcuff you, handicap you, and harass you. The text says that her ex came to the house to get her back.

Some time back, I had a car accident. A month after, Pastor Jeffrey Johnson, Sr., of Eastern Star Baptist Church, and I were preaching in Georgia, for Pastor Marlin Harris.

Pastor Jeffrey Johnson really messed me up the first night, because he used my accident as an illustration in his sermon. My accident had yet to speak to me, but it spoke to Pastor Jeffrey Johnson. He called me that Sunday after he found out that I had not been to church because of the accident. He said, "Man, what happened?" These were my words which he used in his sermon: I said, "Man, I was driving along when the car in front of me stopped because the car in front of it stopped. I looked in my rear view mirror and the car behind me did not stop. I got hit and hurt because what was behind me, caught up to me, and hit me, and that is why I'm in the shape that I'm in right now." Pastor Johnson further added, "Folks, if you're not careful, it's your past that keeps making you do what you don't want to do; it's your past that keeps making you make choices that you wish you had not made. Objects in the mirror may be closer than they appear."

II. THE SYMPTOMS THAT HURT

There is a sickness that handicaps us, but, then **there are symptoms that hurt us.** What I want to do is look at some symptoms in the text, because as you follow the story, this woman's past catches up with her. Now, think about this: the text refers to the man as "husband," but calls her "concubine." I don't understand that. The text calls her father the "father-in-law," but calls her "concubine." I don't understand that kind of double standard that exists right there. If she is called a "concubine," shouldn't he be called a "concubiner"?

The text says that something crazy happens in that they are at the father-in-law's house, they stay for five days, and then the husband says, it's time for us to go. It's late in the evening when they get ready to go, and shortly after they begin to travel, the sun goes down. They come to a city, where they are hoping for hospitality, and the Bible says they go to the town square. In biblical antiquity, hospitality was of supreme value and so when people saw others who were in need of a place to stay, they would open up their homes to them. This town did not do that. And just as the man is about to give up, an old man comes along and says, you can stay with me. So they go to the old man's house. When they get there they begin eating, drinking, and having a good time. Judges 19:22 says: ***While they were enjoying themselves, some of the wicked men of the city surrounded the house. Pounding on the door, they shouted to the old man who owned the house, "Bring out the man who came to your house so we can have sex with him."***

The men say, there is a man in your house, he is some "new meat" from some other town, and since there is "new meat" in town, we want to have sex with him. When you read the Bible it was not "man" singular, there were "men" plural, who wanted to have sex with one man. Evidently, they wanted to pull a train or gang rape the brother. But the bottom-line is, these men wanted this man.

In Judges 19:23-24 we are told: ***The owner of the house went outside and said to them, "No, my friends, don't be so vile. Since this man is my guest, don't do this disgraceful thing. Look, here is my virgin daughter, and his concubine. I will bring them out to you now, and you can use them and do to them whatever you wish. But to this man, don't do such a disgraceful thing."*** This man volunteered his own virgin daughter and then he volunteered his guest's concubine. The brothers were so desirous that the Bible said they insisted, and the Levite, who was in praise rehearsal on Tuesday, kicks his concubine out of the house. And the text says, they gang raped her and they abused her all night long. ***"But the men would not listen to him. So the man took his concubine and sent her outside to them, and they raped her and abused her throughout the night, and at dawn they let her go."***

There are some things that we have to take a good look at by way of symptoms, because there are some sicknesses that are going on in our communities. As a matter of fact, in case you think this kind of stuff isn't happening in the world in which we live, you are in for a rude awakening. It's a sick world in which we find ourselves. Pedophiles are roaming our streets, and they are taking advantage of our innocent, lonely children, many by way of the internet. These pedophiles are taking and raping our children. There is a sickness going on in our time and it has gotten out of control. When it is harnessed and controlled, sex is like electricity—it will light up a room. However, when it is out of control, it will electrocute you.

The text lets us know that this sister, who began as a sex object, finds herself dying as a sex object. Understand, Marvin Gaye sees the only way for him to medicate his misery is through sex, and so Marvin Gaye sings, "When I get that feeling." He wants sexual healing. Why? Because if you're not careful, you will look for sex, the sex that hurts you, as the same source that you think can heal you.

How many one-night stands have you had that you wish you had not had, and the only reason you had them was because of where you were emotionally at that time? If you had not been so wounded, if there had not been an emptiness going on in your life, and if you sought to sexually medicate that emptiness, which could only be healed by a spiritual remedy, then when you did that, you found yourself exacerbating your own emotional dysfunctionality. In many instances, we look for sex to medicate that which was caused by dysfunctional sex.

I remember once I took my daughter, Abeni, with me on a trip to Fairfield, California, and while we were there we went to Six Flags. At Six Flags, we came across this display of snakes, and this one particular snake tripped me out. It was a very small snake, but it caught its prey by putting its tail through dirt, or through grass, or brush, and then the end of the tail comes up through the brush and it looks like a worm. Its prey sees what it thinks is a worm, and wanting to satisfy its hunger, it goes after the tail only to discover at the end of the tail is a snake. Maybe it is not you, but you know of somebody, who went after the tail, but ended up with a snake. The tail looked good, the tail felt good, but that person just didn't know that at the end of the tail was a snake. Sisters, be careful, because at the end of the tail there just might be a snake.

This is what is so bad—sexual healing will never substitute for spiritual healing. The Bible says that this thing was such a hot mess, that the man, having no respect for his concubine, tells her to "get up" after she had been used and abused all night. He shows no concern for her. He just tells her to get up. She does not move, so he picks her up, puts her across his donkey, and the text says he takes her home, cuts her up into twelve pieces, and then sends the twelve pieces to the twelve tribes in Israel. What a sad, sick day!

Then the text closes with this in verse thirty: *Everyone who saw it said, "Such a thing has never been seen or done, not since the day the Israelites came up out of Egypt. Think about it! Consider it! Tell us what to do!"*

III. THE SOLUTION THAT HEALS

The Bible lets us know that not only is there a sickness that handicaps; not only are there symptoms that hurt; but the good news is **there is a solution that heals**. The solution that heals simply says, regardless of how dysfunctional sex may have been in your life, you serve a

God Who is the God of another chance. You serve a God Who says, ***"Therefore, if anyone is in Christ, he is a new creation; the old has gone, the new has come!"*** God is so wonderfully good that He will let you come to the end of yourself where you've done all you can do—you've tried to heal yourself; you've tried to fix yourself; and all of a sudden you realize you can't do this. That is where God wants to get us—to the point where we say, "God, I've tried everything on my own. Is there anything You can do for me?"

That is my word to you. God is saying "quit looking to somebody else. Quit looking for your own cure!" God says, "I want you to reach a point where you're so desperate that the only thing you can do is look up to Me and say, God, if I don't get healed by You, I will not get healed." Have you ever been there? Can you testify that life has knocked you down, but when you were down, you didn't stay down, but you "looked up to the hills from whence comes your help, your help comes from the Lord"?

Here is the power of this passage: the Bible lets us know that this particular section is the last section of the book of Judges which means that Judges, as a book, comes to an end. But, the story of Israel doesn't come to an end, because God will close the book on what broke you, so you can write a sequel of how God saved you.

That is where you may be right now. You are going into your sequel. You know what it's like to be in the last book.

Everything has not always been fine, but God is allowing you to write a brand new sequel. What happened was then, but this is now. And just because you've done that, doesn't mean you are that. You are what God made you and God has done something brand new with you.

We have some wonderful young folks who come to our church on Monday nights. I was up there for praise dance one night, and one of our young folk who I just love, was acting as though she didn't see me, and so, I was acting as though I didn't see her either. Finally, she came up to me and said, "Oh, so you are going to act brand new." I kind of like that and I replied to her, "I am brand new." God saved me; I am brand new. God made me a new man; I am brand new. Once you are brand new, you allow your spirituality to set the standard for your sexuality. When your spirituality sets the standard for your sexuality, then the bottom-line is, you are a person of standards. So, you can say, "don't come to me like that. You can't mistreat me like that. I have standards. It's my spirituality that sets the standards in my sexuality."

When your spirituality sets the standard for your sexuality, that means God gives you spiritual value that makes you a person of high value. When I recognize I'm a person of high value, because of my brand new spiritual value, then my spirituality dictates my sexuality and my theology and Christology dictates my biology.

The text says that he sent out his message and the message

was: What are we going to do? Now, please understand, when you read Judges, especially at the end, there is a recurring theme. The theme is, in those days, everyone did what was right in their own eyes because there was no king in Israel. As a matter of fact, at the end of the book of Judges, it closes with these words: *"In those days, everybody did what was right in their eyes because there was no king in Israel."* The problem was they had no king. And the text implies that until they got a king they were going to go wrong. They needed a king. They wouldn't get healed until they got a king.

I have a wonderful teenage daughter (and it's killing me to watch my baby grow up). In fact, we were on a trip last week, and we were having a wonderful time. I brought my prayer journal along, and as I was going through the prayer journal, I came across a time when Abeni was only three years old. On that particular day, as I recorded in my prayer journal, I was reading Humpty Dumpty to her.

Humpty-Dumpty sat on a wall;
Humpty-Dumpty had a great fall;
All the king's horses and all the king's men
Couldn't put Humpty Dumpty back together again.

I recited that to Abeni, and she started crying. She said, "Is that it? Humpty is dead?" I can't handle my baby crying like that, and so I had to think fast. I came up with a conclusion to Humpty Dumpty.

> Humpty-Dumpty sat on a wall;
> Humpty-Dumpty had a great fall;
> All the king's horses and all the king's men
> Tried and tried and tried,
> But they couldn't put Humpty, back together again.
> And then just when they thought all hope was gone,
> They called for the king who was sitting on the throne,
> And the king came through
> And put Humpty Dumpty back together again.

I told Abeni that the king's horses couldn't do it, the king's men couldn't do it, but the king knew how to do it. I don't know about you, but when my life was in shambles, when my life was a hot mess, ***"God so loved the world that He gave His only begotten Son."*** He sent the King to die for me and to die for you. I have a brand new life now, because the King has put me back together again. There is a King Who will put you back together again, Who will raise you up when you're bent down, Who will put your broken life back together again.

So, Marvin Gaye, sexual healing may feel good, but leave me broken. I need the Saviour's healing because when the Saviour heals you, you are truly healed. And when the Son sets you free, you are free indeed!

Why is Loving You Hurting Me?

When the LORD saw that Leah was not loved, he opened her womb, but Rachel was barren. Leah became pregnant and gave birth to a son. She named him Reuben, for she said, "It is because the LORD has seen my misery. Surely my husband will love me now." She conceived again, and when she gave birth to a son she said, "Because the LORD heard that I am not loved, he gave me this one too." So she named him Simeon. Again she conceived, and when she gave birth to a son she said, "Now at last my husband will become attached to me, because I have borne him three sons." So he was named Levi. She conceived again, and when she gave birth to a son she said, "This time I will praise the LORD." So she named him Judah. Then she stopped having children.

—Genesis 29:31-35

Have you ever had a wonderful dream hijacked by a heartbreaking nightmare? The nightmare rendered you helpless, and before you knew it, you were hopeless, as no exit seemed to hang over the door of your nightmarish situation. Have you ever had something to begin so right and yet, somehow take a devastatingly wrong turn, and

95

in spite of every attempt on your part to make things turn out right, things kept getting worse and worse?

Every now and then, regardless of who you are, you can begin with high hopes and yet things go devastatingly wrong, so much so that it appears that what began as a noble dream has been hijacked by a negative nightmare. And for some of you, that is really how life has turned out.

Well, let me see if I can make this plain by focusing the lens even more. There is no sadder story than the one of Tamar, found in the thirteenth chapter of second Samuel. Tamar is the daughter of King David, and Tamar happens to be extremely beautiful, yet, Tamar soon discovered that the beauty she had going for her ended up being used against her. I think I'll park here, parenthetically, because for some of you, what you have going for you has been sadly used against you. Perhaps it's the way God has blessed you to look; perhaps it's the education you have been blessed to achieve; but whatever the case, it is some gift that God has blessed you with, that sadly, has turned out to be something that haters and others are using against you. This happens to Tamar. The Book says that she is exceedingly beautiful and yet, her beauty gets her in trouble. Why? Because she has a half-brother, by the name of Amnon, and Amnon begins to lust after her. Amnon is so crazy with lust for Tamar that the Bible says: *he became sick because of his love for her.* Amnon is a sick man because Amnon wants to have his own sister. Sick people do sick things that will infect and affect others who are around them.

You may know what it's like to be sick and you may be doing things that are making you sick. Not only are you making yourself sick, but your "sickness" is infecting and affecting others that you supposedly care about. Not only is Amnon sick, but to heal this sickness, he consults with his street smart cousin, who tells him how to get with his own sister. He lets his father, David, know that he is sick, and he wants his sister, David's daughter, to come and feed him out of her hand. The Bible says that David allows Tamar to go to her sick brother, and when she got there Amnon made her cook the food that he desired. As soon as the food was ready, the Bible says that Amnon had everybody put out; he then went into his bedroom and called in Tamar. Tamar innocently went into the room of Amnon and he raped her.

Can you not hear the helpless screams of Tamar as she says, please don't do this? This is a terrible thing to do. But being physically stronger than Tamar, Amnon because of his sickness, takes advantage of Tamar. Imagine how Tamar must have felt. She must have felt something similar to what Ludacris articulates in the song, "Runaway Love," about poor little Lisa:

> *Lisa is stuck up in the world on her own;*
> *Forced to think that hell is a place called home.*

For some of you, the one thing you don't want to do is go home. As a matter of fact, for some people the one place they look forward to not going to is home. Some of you spend as much time away from home as you can because of the hell you are catching at home. Why? Because I've discovered that hell is not merely an eschatological destination that you will go to after you die if you are without Christ; hell can be an existential situation that you find yourself in, even if you love Christ. In other words, hell can come to you right where you live. That is what happened to Tamar. Tamar is a victim of domestic violence and sexual assault. I'm dealing with this because sadly and shamefully, domestic violence has become the pink elephant in the living room of the African-American community. Some of us go to church, Sunday after Sunday, not realizing that there are people in our pews, sitting there, silently suffering. Yes, they are praising God, but they are internally shattered and broken by the hell they are catching at home.

Let me see if I can make this plain to you. I read an interesting story about this sister over in Austria. She went to a hospital for abdominal surgery. When she got to the hospital, she went through prep and all of that stuff, and then it was time for the surgery. They gave her a muscle relaxer to relax the muscles in her body and she soon found herself incapable of moving. A machine was placed adjacent to the bed, and it was supposed to release the anesthesia that was going to put her to sleep. Forty-five minutes into the surgery, a doctor walked in and noticed that the lady was lying there with tears flowing down her cheeks. He then noticed that someone had forgotten to hook the machine up so that it could release the anesthesia into her body. Consequently, for forty-five minutes this lady had been opened up and because the muscle relaxer was already working in her system, all she could do was lay there and silently suffer. Can you not hear her silent screams as she is immobilized, incarcerated in her own pain? Can you not feel her pain even right now as she sees no exit out of her painful predicament?

God may have you reading this chapter for a reason. Why? Because you may be silently suffering; nobody knows the trouble you've seen; nobody knows your sorrow. Even though you may be a saint in the sanctuary, even though you are a Christian in church, you are a suffering saint because you are being victimized by domestic violence and abuse.

You might be asking, "well, what is domestic violence and what does it look like?" Notice, if you will, that *domestic violence and abuse* comes when one is trying to dominate another and will exert a power that is designed to render the person incapable of getting out of that situation. Domestic violence means you have been so violated, physically, psychologically, emotionally, economically, or even spiritually, that you feel you are handcuffed by helplessness and there is no way out of the situation in which you find yourself.

Sometimes domestic violence manifests itself physically, in that the *physical abuse* is either directly or indirectly coming in your direction. By indirectly, we mean the abuser throws objects, not at you, but around you. They are so volatile in their temper that it literally renders you psychologically fearful, and you find yourself wondering if the violence is ever going to come your way. Now, there is also direct violence where somebody has been physically hit, hurt, and wounded by somebody they thought loved them and who they certainly thought they loved. They were supposed to take care of you, yet, they begin to hurt you—physically.

So, there is physical abuse, but then there is also *psychological abuse.* Psychological abuse is when you live under the threat all of the time of being hurt or wounded. Psychological abuse has many manifestations, such as neglect or rejection.

Not only is there psychological abuse, but there is also *economic abuse,* where one person is controlling the money. The abuser is a control freak. He has to control somebody, and so he controls you, sometimes economically.

And then other times they will attempt to control you *spiritually.* You see that is why you have to be careful about believing that if you find somebody in the church you found your Heaven-sent man or woman. The Bible says that a tree is known by the fruit it bears. So I don't care if they go to church; if they are not bearing the *"fruit of the spirit"*—love, joy, peace, long suffering, etc., that is not the man or woman for you. Someone who engages in spiritual abuse will literally use the Bible, the Word of God, to control you and to keep you in your place. They will know just enough Scripture to use it as a weapon on you, as opposed to using it to edify you.

Abuse and domestic violence go on much too often in our community. We are a community of the walking wounded—of persons who have been abused as elders, for there is elderly abuse as well. In too many of our nursing homes, our seniors are sadly and sinfully abused. In too many instances, we have children who have been physically and emotionally abused. And then there is the abuse that goes on between couples.

That is what I'm dealing with because that is the pink elephant in the living room of our community. Sadly, churches have stuck their heads in the sand, while we have members who are suffering in silence, believing that they can claim their way out of their situation, when in reality, they need some help, they need some healing, they need some treatment, and they need some support.

Let me strongly say here, there is no shame in getting some counseling. There is no shame in getting some help. The shame is to stay in a situation where you are abusing someone, or you are being abused. You do have a choice. You can make a decision. Nothing has to stay the way it is unless you give your permission.

Our text is an interesting and insightful case study of domestic violence or abuse. You say there is no physical abuse in this passage. You are right. Even though Leah was not physically abused, she was physically violated. I will come to that matter a little later, because by way of context, Leah's nightmare began when Jacob fell in love with her sister, Rachel.

The Bible lets us know that Jacob came to a well, and a honey, by the name of Rachel, came up, and Jacob was so in love with how this woman looked and carried herself, he let it be known that he wanted to hook up with her. The Bible tells us that Laban, her father, said, "before you can have my baby girl, you are going to have to work seven years." Jacob was glad to work for Rachel, but at the end of the seven years, Jacob found himself in a bad situation.

Why? Because the wedding party is on, and evidently Jacob had had too many trips to the bowl where they were serving wine. The Book lets us know that Jacob did not know that his uncle, Laban, had switched sisters on him. So, instead of ending up in his wedding bed that night with Rachel, he wakes up the next day only to discover that he had slept with Leah, and not Rachel.

Imagine how Leah must have felt to be put in a situation with a man who did not want her. But here is the bad thing—Leah's abuse began because her father set her up to be in a relationship that brought her down. Sisters, if you are not careful, and you do not properly process the relationship that you had or did not have with your father, you will become a magnet for men who come in your life and bring about the same pain and hurt that your father brought in your life and in the life of your mother. It all began because Laban set her up to be brought down. Laban, how low-down can you be? Why would you set your daughter up to be brought down? Why would you set your daughter up to be rejected?

Fathers, you need to recognize your important responsibility, and that is, you are marking your child's future. If you have a daughter, that daughter falls in love with you first, and then that daughter sees you as the model for all of the men that will later come in her life. If she sees a low model, then she is going to have low men attracted to her. So brothers, I don't care what you feel about your baby's mama, it's time to step up and handle your business because we have to save our future generations from further abuse.

As I moved through the text, it kept bothering me, because Leah was in this bad situation and the question is: Leah, what do you do when you get in a bad situation such as this? The text says Leah was unloved. Genesis 29:31 says: **When the LORD saw that Leah was not loved, he opened her womb, but Rachel was barren.** I looked up the Hebrew rendering for 'not loved' and the Hebrew word is much stronger. The Hebrew word says that Leah was "hated." As a matter of fact, the word for "hate" means that she was violently hated. She was so violently hated that she experienced Jacob not wanting to be in her presence. She's a victim of domestic violence and domestic abuse. The question again is: Leah, what do you do when you are in a situation like that? Look at what Leah does. Leah tried to exchange sexual healing to get a loving feeling.

That is what sisters often do. Sisters wrongfully believe that if they give up the sex, then somehow the man will start to love her. No, brothers are not wired like that. Brothers are wired in such a way that when sex is going down, all they are concerned about is that good feeling that sex gives them. Once they have achieved that good feeling, as far as they are concerned, it is time to turn over and go to sleep. Why? Because it was about reaching that climax, and once he gets what he wants, his mentality is: hit it, quit it, and forget it.

So the Bible says that Leah gave him sex. Genesis 29:32 says: **Leah became pregnant and gave birth to a son. She named him Reuben, for she said, "It is because the LORD has seen my misery. Surely my husband will love me now."** Of course, after the sex came the pregnancy. Many sisters believe that maybe if he gets me pregnant, I can keep him. First, Leah gave him some. Then, she got pregnant. Then, she had a baby. But the text lets us know that nothing Leah did changed how Jacob felt about her. Sisters, I don't care how much you give him sex; I don't care if you have a baby by him, that is not going to keep him. As a matter of fact, that is going to drive him further away from you. Quit trying to use sex to keep a man! Quit trying to get pregnant to keep a man! It does not work.

Hold on, it gets worse. The text says, she keeps having baby after baby after baby. She doesn't just have one. She keeps going back for more and more and more. Why? Because there is a cycle going on here. Whenever you are a victim of abuse, you always get caught up in a cycle. Do you see the cycle in the text? The text says that she sleeps with him, gets pregnant by him, and hopes he'll love her, he does not love her; so she sleeps with him again, gets pregnant by him, and hopes he'll love her, but he does not love her; so she sleeps with him, gets pregnant by him, and so forth. My question to you is: Are you in a cycle where you keep going through the same old stuff, and ending up at the same old place?

The good news is: that cycle can be broken. There is healing and there is hope. The choice is yours to make a change. I'm not saying change him or change her, because quiet as it's kept, there are men who have also been abused; there are men who have been neglected and rejected as well. But the good news today is: You can choose to experience change. You can't change them, but you can allow God to change you. And once God changes you, hopefully, you will then begin to make choices that will bring about a permanent change.

Some of you may still be thinking about the woman I wrote about who was forty-five minutes into surgery, without any pain medication. Well, the good news is: her situation changed. How? The doctor came in and after noticing that the pain machine was not hooked up, he hooked her up. Not only that, but the doctor helped her to get a settlement of over $100,000.00. In a real sense, her situation changed when the doctor came in.

I want you to know that I serve a God Who is so good; He is a Doctor in the sick room. And if you let the Doctor come in, the Doctor will hook you up. Have you been hooked up by my Doctor? He'll make you feel better— that's the hookup. He'll make you stronger—that's the hookup. He'll give you peace—that's the hookup. He'll give you joy—that's the hookup. He'll give you love— that's the hookup. He'll give you power—that's the hookup!

Let me leave with you three things that I know will bless you.

I. WHEN YOU ARE GOING THROUGH THE BAD, GOD WILL BLESS YOU IN IT SO THAT YOU CAN STILL GET SOME GOOD OUT OF IT

The text lets us know that **when you are going through the bad, God will bless you in it, so that you can still**

get some good out of it.

Have you ever looked back over past situations and it seems as though God gave you just enough to get through each day? You should have gone crazy; you should have gone coastal or ballistic; but instead, God kept giving you just enough grace to bring you through.

Have you ever had some time relief medicine? Time relief medicine releases its medication just when the pain starts to hurt. God has a way of giving us time relief blessings. God says: I know you're hurting right now, but I'm going to give you just enough to get you through the day. As the Psalmist said: "Morning by morning new mercies I see." God is so faithful and He knows what is coming in my day; when I wake up in the morning God has already injected me with just enough mercy to handle what's bringing me misery.

The text says, ***"but because Leah was hated, the Lord."*** When the Lord saw that Leah was being abused, the Lord said, I'm going to do something for you that I am not doing for other folks. I'm going to give you something that will elevate your status in this sick situation. And the Bible says the Lord opened up her womb and she became pregnant.

Now, let me tell you something, I'm so glad that James Cone radically transformed theology in the '60s because James Cone looked at American theology, which was a theology from the top down, and said, "You all got it wrong. When I read the Bible, I don't see God as a top-down God, I see God as a bottom-up God." And God is the God of the oppressed. God always sides with those who are abused, misused, and downtrodden. I am sorry for anybody who thinks that God is on their side because they're on top. No, when you read Scripture, God always showed up on the side of the Hebrew and Egyptian slaves. God shows up on the side of those who are underdogs and so you can't even read our history without testifying if it had not been for the Lord on our side. You may be living in a home where the situation is unfavorable for you. Here is what God is saying to you: "I'm going to come on your side, and make a difference."

While growing up at Third Baptist Church under my father's pastoralship, Cazzie Russell joined our church. Cazzie Russell played for the Golden State Warriors. He was a 3-point shooter before there was a 3-point shot. The boy was just bad. Cazzie would come to the gym while we were playing basketball on Monday nights. We had teams at the church and we would play each other often. We would have a wonderful time of fellowship, where we got to grow and to know each other.

One day, we are playing a game and the team that I'm on was getting spanked. I mean, it was downright abusive what the other team was doing to us. Cazzie is standing on the sidelines trying to give us pointers on how to play the game. Seeing that my team is getting abused, he calls timeout, and says to us, "Listen, for the rest of the game, I'm going to play on this team." With Cazzie on our side, immediately the game began to shift. We began to run faster because we knew if Cazzie was passing us the ball, all we had to do was be in the right place at the right time, and Cazzie would get an assist and we would get a lay up. And then, when our shots weren't falling, we knew if we just passed the ball to Cazzie that Cazzie would make shots that we couldn't make ourselves. Cazzie made all of us better. Cazzie made our game elevate, to the point of us winning the game that we were suppose to lose. When did the game shift? It shifted when Cazzie got on our side.

If you feel you are losing, your game can shift when you let the Lord in on your side, because when God is on your side, God will elevate your game. God will elevate your expectations.

II. IN THE MIDST OF YOUR ABUSIVE SITUATION, GOD BLESSES YOU IN IT BY ALLOWING YOU TO GIVE BIRTH TO SOMETHING NEW

The text says that Leah gave birth. Here's your treatment. **Your treatment lets you know that in the midst of your abusive situation, God blesses you in it, by allowing you to give birth to something new, even through labor pains**. The text says that she gave birth to something new. Only God can use the hell you're going through to do something brand new for you that you would not have experienced had you not been through that hell.

Some of you are where you are right now, not because you have chosen to be there, but because you have gone through enough hell, where God had to shut some doors in order for him to usher you into where you are right now. God does not want you to suffer, but He is allowing your suffering and He is using your abuse to bring you to where you need to be.

Have you ever heard the story about that little girl who was desperately afraid of a storm as it raged one night, and how she kept calling for her Daddy? Daddy came in the room and she said, "Daddy, I'm afraid of the storm." Daddy said, "Baby, I'm right there." She said, "Well, Daddy, will you hold me through the storm." And Daddy said, "Of course I will, baby." And Daddy held his baby girl through the storm. When the morning dawned, the storm had passed over and had given way to a brilliant, radiant sunlight. As the sunlight came into her room through the window, the little girl couldn't help but look up and say, "Daddy, look at what a beautiful day it is. Can you believe as bad as last night was that today is so beautiful?"

And Daddy said, "Yes, baby." Here is her insightful interpretation: "Daddy, you know what happened? You held me through the storm and God used the storm to make way for the beautiful day."

When I heard that story, it dawned on me that the little

girl was on to something, and that is: only God can hold you in the midst of what is messing with you. And while God is holding you, God is using the storm to set the stage for a brand new day. The Psalmist tells us that: *Weeping may endure for a night, but joy cometh in the morning.*

Psychologists and counselors say that whenever you're in an abusive situation, you are in a cycle: (1) honeymoon— where everyone is happy; everything feels good. (2) After the honeymoon stage, they say there's the kitchen stage. The kitchen is when the relationship begins to build; the finger is on the trigger; the gun has been cocked, and so it's tension now. (3) But, then you move beyond tension to explosion, (4) and after explosion there is apology. After apology, you go back to honeymoon. But then honeymoon gives way to tension, tension then gives way to explosion, explosion then gives way to apology, and apology becomes honeymoon.

Have you been through this kind of thing? You knew the honeymoon was good, but then the tension has you on edge. As a matter of fact, you can't even enjoy the honeymoon because you don't know when the honeymoon is going to give way to tension.

The text says in Genesis 29:32-34: *Leah became pregnant and gave birth to a son. She named him Reuben, for she said, "It is because the LORD has seen my misery. Surely my husband will love me now." She conceived again, and when she gave birth to a son she said, "Because the LORD heard that I am not loved, he gave me this one too." So she named him Simeon. Again she conceived, and when she gave birth to a son she said, "Now at last my husband will become attached to me, because I have borne him three sons." So he was named Levi.* When she has her fourth child, she says, "you know what, bunk Jacob, now I'm going to praise God." Genesis 29:35: *She conceived again, and when she gave birth to a son she said, "This time I will praise the LORD." So she named him Judah. Then she stopped having children.*

Let me help you here because this is very important—you can't change Jacob. I don't care how much sex you give him, how many gifts you buy him, how compliant you are around him—you cannot change Jacob! Jacob is who Jacob is. Only God can change Jacob. Quit trying to change somebody, because the only way you can qualify to change somebody is you have got to lead a perfect life, die on the cross, and rise from the dead.

Jacob is who he is because he got it from his daddy. Jacob got his identity from home. So, you are trying to change what he got from home. Remember, Jacob means "conniving, scheming trickster." He was given that name by his family, and spent the rest of his life living down to the identity his family gave him. Only when God met him by the river and changed him by wrestling with him all night long, did Jacob change. So quit trying to do what is only in God's job description. You can't change Jacob, but you can change your mind.

Do you see what happened here? The text says that she changed her mind. I love the treatment process of God. God gives her treatment because every time she has a child, except for when she had Levi, she connects it with God. The unfortunate thing was that she named her children according to her pain. She marked and stamped her children based upon how she was being abused. If your situation is abusive, please get out of there. Why? Because it's not just you, your child may suffer as well; your child is being abused also, your child is being marked and marred also.

She connects her misery with God: *"Reuben—the Lord has noticed my misery;"* Simeon—*"the Lord heard I was unloved;"* Judah—*"praise the Lord."* How did the cycle get broken? The cycle got broken when she shifted her focus from trying to get love from Jacob to just praising the Lord. It dawned on her: "you know what, I can't change him, but I can change me. To change me, I'm going to hook up with the God above me." The text says, she just began to praise the Lord.

III. PRAISE WILL ALTER YOUR DISPOSITION SO THAT YOU CAN OVERCOME YOUR ABUSIVE SITUATION

Praise will alter your disposition so that you can overcome your abusive situation. Keep on going to church, keep on praising God, because there is power in praise. I don't know about you, but sometimes I go to church not feeling my best, but then the choir sings my song, the preacher preaches my message, and God uses the praise to heal me.

I love this. Leah names him Judah, and out of the tribe of Judah, came the Lion of Judah. The Lion of Judah was born in Bethlehem, raised in Nazareth, ministered in a desert place, died one dark Friday, and when He died, He was abused, but God used His abuse for my healing. *He was wounded for my transgressions, bruised for my iniquity, the chastisement of our peace was upon Him, and with His stripes, we are healed.*

Leah names him Judah. The word in Hebrew is *Yehudah*. It means "praise leads to thanksgiving." What does she have to be thankful for? Her husband doesn't love her, but that isn't her focus any more. And once your focus changes, God gives you a new outlook, and the outlook changes how you feel on the inside. Once you change what's on the inside, you change your outlook, and you know you are going to have a better outcome. So, just begin to thank God in the midst of the stuff you are going through and for the stuff that God is doing for you. In the midst of the stuff, thank God for watching over you; thank God you still have your right mind; thank God for a reasonable portion of health and strength. In spite of the tragedies that are going on around us, all I can say is, "thank you, Lord, for all You have done for me. Thank

You for watching over me. Thank You for taking good care of me."

Yadah is "praise that leads to thanksgiving." Yadah also means "to extend your hands." Guess what: You use your hands in other areas of your life. You use your hands to express when you're mad; You use your hands to express when you're happy; You use your hands to express when you don't feel good; so why don't you use your hands to say "thank you"?

My best memories of Abeni Jewel, my daughter, are from when she was my little baby. I won't forget one time she had fallen down and was hurt. Guess what she did? Abeni did not just sit there trying to be sophisticated, cultivated, and dignified. Abeni knew her Daddy was in the atmosphere, and so knowing that, she held up both hands. Guess what? I did not say, "You little charismatic. Shame on you for holding up your hands. Put your hands down!" No, my baby was wounded and was holding up those hands. By holding up her hands, she was simply saying, I want to be closer to you. By holding up those hands, she was saying, I can't handle this hurt by myself. By holding up those hands, she was saying, If I can just get close to you, I know I'll feel a whole lot better. And when she held up those hands, I rushed to my baby, I picked her up, and once I picked her up, guess what? She stopped crying all together. She was still wounded, but she was in Daddy's arms. She was still hurting, but she was in Daddy's arms.

Have you been hurt or wounded? I dare you to hold up your hands to God, and say, "thank You for being my Father. Thank You for watching over me. Thank You. Now I need You like never before." He will pick you up He will turn you around. Don't be discouraged because: **"joy comes in the morning."** God is standing by. There's healing for your sorrow. There's healing for your pain. There is a balm in Gilead. ***"He was wounded for my transgressions."*** God will heal you!

THERE'S SOME MUSIC WE JUST CAN'T DANCE TO

Furious with rage, Nebuchadnezzar summoned Shadrach, Meshach and Abednego. So these men were brought before the king, and Nebuchadnezzar said to them, "Is it true, Shadrach, Meshach and Abednego, that you do not serve my gods or worship the image of gold I have set up? Now when you hear the sound of the horn, flute, zither, lyre, harp, pipes and all kinds of music, if you are ready to fall down and worship the image I made, very good. But if you do not worship it, you will be thrown immediately into a blazing furnace. Then what god will be able to rescue you from my hand?"

Shadrach, Meshach and Abednego replied to the king, "O Nebuchadnezzar, we do not need to defend ourselves before you in this matter. If we are thrown into the blazing furnace, the God we serve is able to save us from it, and he will rescue us from your hand, O king. But even if he does not, we want you to know, O king, that we will not serve your gods or worship the image of gold you have set up."

Then Nebuchadnezzar was furious with Shadrach, Meshach and Abednego, and his attitude toward them changed. He ordered the furnace heated seven times hotter than usual and commanded some of the strongest soldiers in his army to tie up Shadrach, Meshach and Abednego and throw them into the blazing furnace. So these men, wearing their robes, trousers, turbans and other clothes, were bound and thrown into the blazing furnace. The king's command was so urgent and the furnace so hot that the flames of the fire killed the soldiers who took up Shadrach, Meshach and Abednego, and these three men, firmly tied, fell into the blazing furnace.

Then King Nebuchadnezzar leaped to his feet in amazement and asked his advisers, "Weren't there three men that we tied up and threw into the fire?" They replied, "Certainly, O king."

He said, "Look! I see four men walking around in the fire, unbound and unharmed, and the fourth looks like a son of the gods."

Nebuchadnezzar then approached the opening of the blazing furnace and shouted, "Shadrach, Meshach and Abednego, servants of the Most High God, come out! Come here!" So Shadrach, Meshach and Abednego came out of the fire, and the satraps, prefects, governors and royal advisers crowded around them. They saw that the fire had not harmed their bodies, nor was a hair of their heads singed; their robes were not scorched, and there was no smell of fire on them.

Then Nebuchadnezzar said, "Praise be to the God of Shadrach, Meshach and Abednego, who has sent his angel and rescued his servants! They trusted in him and defied the king's command and were willing to give up their lives rather than serve or worship any god except their own God. Therefore I decree that the people of any nation or language who say anything against the God of Shadrach, Meshach and Abednego be cut into pieces and their houses be turned into piles of rubble, for no other god can save in this way."

Then the king promoted Shadrach, Meshach and Abednego in the province of Babylon.

—Daniel 3:13-30

One day, I was watching a documentary, (I believe it was on the Learning Channel), and in this particular documentary, they shared how certain sheep are slaughtered. It's a horrible process. During this process, a Judas goat leads the sheep up the ramp. Now understand when the sheep reach the top of the ramp, and turn right, they turn right to their own slaughter and destruction. This particular Judas goat is trained to walk up the ramp, and once the Judas goat reaches the top of the ramp, it suddenly turns left instead of right. The Judas goat begins his journey up the ramp, looks back at the sheep that are scared and afraid to move; but when they see the boldness of the Judas goat, it dawns on them that if the Judas goat is going up the ramp, the ramp must be all right. So, one by one, these dumb sheep that don't have a mind of their own, simply follow whoever is out in front. They don't think for themselves; they simply do what the rest of the crowd is doing. So the dumb sheep see the goat up on the ramp, and then one by one, they begin to go up the ramp and before they know it, they look up, and the Judas goat has vanished from sight. Unknown to them, the Judas goat has been snatched to the left and when they reach the top, instead of going left, they go right—to their destruction.

What happened to the sheep? The sheep messed up because they did not think for themselves. They trusted someone who had been set up to bring them down.

It was interesting watching Oprah's show one day, and to hear hip-hop artist, Common say, with insight and integrity, that rap music, hip-hop, if you please, has somehow or another taken a wrong turn. Those of us who are hip-hop lovers recognize that hip-hop has revolutionary roots that go all the way back to Gil Scott-Heron. Hip-hop has revolutionary roots in music that confronted, the injustices of the culture, and consequently, in New York, back in the mid-70s, hip-hop became a culture—a culture that was birthed in the environment of pain, poverty, and suffering. Those in the hip-hop community let us know that only God could give black folk creativity out of a crisis. I love that right there, because it lets me know that regardless of what crisis you may find yourself in, God has a way of using the hell that you were going through to bring something out of you that would not have come out of you had you not been through that hell.

Many of you discovered your purpose and your calling, not because you made all of the right choices and decisions, but some of you had to hit your head against the wall, some of you found yourself with your back against the wall, others of you were caught up in a crisis, but then God used a negative situation to bring out of you what He had placed in you.

By 1979, rap first appeared on the stage of public acclaim. The Sugar Hill Gang burst onto the stage, and folks were jamming to this new breed of music. Rap music had taken center stage and the beauty of it is that rap music began as a mirror that would confront the culture about the injustice, racism, poverty, and dysfunction in the African-American community. A mirror is a reflection for correction.

My favorite was Grandmaster Flash and The Furious Five, who looked at the dysfunction caused by racism and injustice, and threw down:

It's like a jungle sometimes
It makes me wonder how I keep from goin' under
It's like a jungle sometimes
It makes me wonder how I keep from goin' under

And then they sung:

Don't push me 'cuz I'm close to the edge
I'm trying not to lose my head

If you keep on living this life, life will push you close to the edge. Life is a jungle that will sometimes make you feel like you're going under. Life has pushed many of us so close to the edge that we feel as though we are about to lose our minds.

I believe it was Chuck D who called rap music the "CNN of black culture." KRS-One called it "edutainment," in that we were educated through the entertainment of rap music. Michael Eric Dyson said that "rappers became our poetic prophets, who spoke truth to power, and dealt with the harsh realities of the hood." Rap music was doing the real thing.

On Oprah, Common said, "rap began right, but somehow it's taken a wrong turn." It's taken a wrong turn, and now sadly, sinfully, and shamefully, we have borrowed the language of oppression to describe ourselves. We have borrowed the language of oppression to continue the dehumanizing of our African-American women. Rap music, when it took a wrong turn, began to sexually objectify our black women, and consequently, black women are being called out of their name. That is beneath the dignity of our sisters. We are using the language of our oppressors, and that means we have become a coconspirator with the folk who never did like us, when we dehumanize and disrespect our black women. I pray that God will give us a new generation who says, we're not going to follow the Judas goat; it's time out for dissing our sisters; it's time out for using the language of oppression. God set us free!

We took a wrong turn, led by a Judas goat, being paid by corporate America. As long as rap music was underground, and we were distributing the music ourselves, we did not allow white corporations to dictate the lyrics and the music that was being sent to our people. And so maybe we need to go back underground, and say, "time out for you making money off of our dysfunction."

It bothers me when I hear rapper, 50 Cent, say he ain't changing the way he talks because rap is a mirror of the culture. It mirrors his reality. He's going to use the language that demeans and dehumanizes our sisters because it's a mirror. I like what Al Sharpton said: "What do you use a mirror for? You don't use a mirror to go look in and talk about my hair ain't combed, so I ain't going to comb it. No, you use a mirror to comb your hair, to get the smit out of your eyes, to brush your teeth, and to make sure when you leave that mirror you leave that mirror better than when you first looked in that mirror." Use the mirror to correct what needs to be corrected.

What really bothers me is that not only has rap taken a wrong turn, but some of us are dancing to the music as it makes a wrong turn. I can't understand how you can be a sister of dignity, and character, and know who you are, and dance to music that calls you out of your name. How can you buy music that calls you out of your own name?

So, then you have a person like Imus, who thought he

was slick, and instead of being repentant, he became a little rebellious, and said, "well, what I said isn't any worse than what their own folks say," as if he got it from rap. He is lying. Our sisters have been mistreated and dissed since the days of the Middle Passage, the heinous horrors of slavery, and the dehumanizing Jim Crow. As a matter of fact, if you saw "ROOTS," you know that the body of an African-American woman did not belong to herself. A black woman was raped, mistreated, and called all out of her name. If you ever meet Imus, tell Imus I said that you did not get it from rappers; you got it from your ancestors. That is where you got it from. So, Imus isn't excused.

Now, black folk, what is our excuse? Why is it that we are borrowing the language of oppression? There's some music we just can't dance to.

Our text tells us that Nebuchadnezzar decided to have this huge image erected. The image is erected, and Nebuchadnezzar says, "I'm going to have some music played, and the moment the music plays, everybody is to bow down to the image and worship it." What Nebuchadnezzar is saying is, "I'm going to use music as an instrument of control. I'm going to use the music that folk move to as an instrument to reinforce oppression. I'm going to use music in my kingdom to reinforce the oppression I am exerting over the nation."

The Bible lets us know in Psalm 137 that the Jews had already given up their music. When the people asked them "why don't you sing some of the songs of Zion," the Bible says they hung their harps on the willows and said, "how are we going to sing the Lord's song in a strange land"? They had given up their music, and now the Bible says Nebuchadnezzar gives some new music that reinforces their oppression. Do you not know that music has that kind of power? Do you not know that music can move you in the right direction, or move you in the wrong direction?

If I mentioned some music like Luther—"A Chair is Still a Chair, Even When There's No One Sittin' There"—immediately, you would have a flashback. And the flashback would remind you of where you were, who you were with, when you did what you did, because you were moved by the music.

What if I go back to the Isley Brothers? The Isley Brothers will mess you up, especially if you have a flashback to those house parties down in the basement. The music had you making some moves that you may not have otherwise made. As a matter of fact, some of you got your rap with the honey you were talking to and slow dancing with. Some of you would just start singing to her, all out of tune, but the bottom line was the music was making you move.

Maybe you can remember some church songs when you came to church one Sunday, and you heard the right song at the right time, and that song put something in your spirit and gave you power to handle the challenges of the week. Music can move you wrong, or music can move you right. But, there's some music you ought not to dance to.

Notice that the text says Nebuchadnezzar has the music to play and when the music plays, everybody bows down except Shadrach, Meshech, and Abednego. I love it because the text lets us know they refused to dance to that kind of music. They weren't going to allow themselves to be controlled by that music. It violated who they were. Recognize that Shadrach, Meshech, and Abednego had been kidnapped, and brought as slaves, into Babylon. Dr. Asa Hillard described to us the slave making process: "Whenever you make a slave, you want it to be complete. First of all, you've got to erase their memory. That means that they have no connection with the heritage from which they come, because if you don't know where you come from, you have no clue as to where you are supposed to go." Asa said, "erase their memory, and then change their identity." That is why you don't know Shadrach, Meshech, and Abednego by their real names, which were Hananiah, Mishael, and Azariah, because their names were changed by the Babylonians who were trying to change their identity. If somebody can tell you who you are, then you will spend your life living down to what they tell you.

Dr. Asa Hilliard goes on to say, "Erase their memory, change their identity, and control their education. Either you don't get an education, or they force feed you a test, so you memorize what you're told instead of being challenged to critically think and analyze for yourself. So, you control their education, and you break up their family." That is what happened to Shadrach, Meshech, and Abednego—memory erased, identity changed, education controlled, and broken from their families. It looks like they were going to be some good slaves. But, I like how Dr. Manuel Scott put it: "When the slave makers tried to make us slaves here, they made one mistake: they let us get to church. Because we got to church, we had a faith that said, 'in spite of you taking my memory, I'm going to replace it with some brand new memory. You may have changed my name, but you can't change who I am, because since I know Whose I am that is going to reinforce who I am, no matter where I am.'"

Shadrach, Meshech, and Abednego said, "you may have changed our name, but you didn't take away our faith." The Book says when Nebuchadnezzar had the music played, they refused to bow down.

Rapper, Nas, raises the question when he asks, "is hip-hop dead?" Nas maintains in its present form that it needs to be destroyed–it has been controlled by corporations, it has been reduced to simply just a few things.

What do we do? What solutions do we have? Let's not follow the Judas goat and go in the wrong direction, but let's correct things. How do we correct things? I'm going to give you three points:

I. YOUR FAITH WILL GIVE YOU STANDARDS ON WHICH TO STAND

The text says when you have faith in God that **faith will give you standards on which to stand.** Faith in God gives you standards that you can stand on. Do you like what Shadrach, Meshech, and Abednego did? Nebuchadnezzar is ticked and says, "I'm going to give you one more chance to bow down and do the right thing. You do it as soon as the music plays." Shadrach, Meshech, and Abednego said, "Oh king, chill. Bring it down, because the bottom line is, you can play the music all you want to, we are not dancing to that music. What you don't understand is, we have standards, and the standards that we stand on will not let us dance to any kind of music."

God deliver me from folk who go through life without any standards, without any boundaries, and without any conditions. You see whenever you really know who you are, and Whose you are, there is some junk you are not going to put up with, and there is some mess you are not going to allow to come your way, because it contradicts your convictions.

They said, "we are not bowing." Their confidence is rooted in their theology. Whose they are defines who they are, no matter who they are up against. The bottom line is, when you are secure in Whose you are, it makes you strong in who you are, and when you are secure in Whose you are, and you are strong in who you are, it really doesn't matter who comes against you, and what they have to say. They can threaten you, they can huff and puff to blow your house down, but, you're like the three little pigs in the house of bricks, and you can say, "huff and puff all you want to, this house is not going to blow down, because we know who we are, we know Whose we are, and it doesn't matter who we are up against. Our God is able." God is able to wipe tears from your eyes. God is able to make a way where there was no way. God is able to make your enemies your footstool. God is able to raise up those who are bowed down. God is able!

So, they say, "God is able to deliver us, and He's going to do it, but if He chooses not to, it isn't going to change what we believe, and since what we believe orders how we behave, we are not going to bow down regardless of what the consequences may be."

God, give us some folk with that kind of faith, and the kind of conviction that says, "you know what, I'm going to serve God whether He comes through or not; I'm going to serve God whether He opens this door this time or not, because the bottom line is, even if God doesn't do it, I know God is able to do it." Regardless of how things may turn out, your attitude should be: I know God is able even if He doesn't do it this time. God is able to make a way even if He doesn't make a way this time. For some of you, your thing is, if God can make a way, you want Him to always make a way, but God isn't like that.

God is so awesomely sovereign that He says, "I don't have to make a way in order to show you how awesome I am. As a matter of fact, I'll let you get in the situation." The bottom line is, you ought to have some standards that you stand on. Knowing when you stand on standards, you are not standing by yourself.

II. FAITH RELEASES GOD TO SHOW UP AND SHOW OUT

After you have standards that you stand on, rooted in your faith, you discover that **faith releases God to show up and show out.** Do you not know that your lack of faith puts handcuffs on God? Do you not know that you can literally tie God's hands to the point where He can't do what He would otherwise do if you simply had faith?

The Bible says: Jesus, Heaven's Hero and earth's Emancipator; Jesus, Who healed the sick, raised the dead, open blinded eyes; Jesus, Who did some impossible stuff like walking on the water, could do no mighty works in His own hood of Nazareth, because of the people's unbelief. Because they did not have faith, they literally handcuffed the Lord; they tied the hands of Jesus. Your lack of faith will cause you to get in the way of what God wants to do for you.

Shadrach, Meshech, and Abednego said, "we aren't going to bow down." Nebuchadnezzar is ticked, and he is so ticked that he doesn't wait for sentencing; he doesn't wait for a jury. Nebuchadnezzar orders the strongest men in the kingdom to tie them up, and to throw them in the fire. But before he does that, he turns the furnace up seven times hotter than normal.

See, my thing is, "okay God, I took a stand for You, and now I'm in this fire." That is where you may be right now. You've been trying to do the right thing, and you thought that God, in light of you trying to do the right thing, would at least keep you out of some stuff. Sometimes, it seems as though God will actually let you get in the fire, but by faith, God says when you are in that fire, you are not in there by yourself.

My mentor, Jeremiah 'Daddy J' Wright said that "God is watching what is unfolding up in glory" and He convenes His angelic counsel and says to the angels, "check this out. My boys are about to get thrown in the fire and I need somebody to get down there real fast, because I can't have my boys hurt." And all of a sudden, Gabriel says, "God, let me go. I will handle that thing." God says, "Well, how long will it take you, Gabriel, to get there?" Gabriel said, "God give me ninety seconds; I'll be in the fire, and they will be set free." God said, "Ninety seconds? Did you just see what Nebuchadnezzar did? He turned that bad boy up seven times hotter than normal and when he threw them in, those who threw them in got burnt up themselves. We can't wait ninety seconds." Michael said, "God, Gabriel is too slow. Let me jump in there." God said, "how long will it take you to get from Heaven to earth?" Michael said, "Give me thirty seconds; I'll be in the fire." God said, "No, that takes too long." They said, "God, what are you going to do?" He said, "I'm going to handle this bad boy myself." "Well, God, how long will it take You to get there?" "Look, I'm already there."

Whatever fire you're in, God is in there with you. Why do you think you're still alive? Why do you think you haven't lost your mind by now? Because God has been in the fire with you.

These Hebrew boys were walking in what was supposed to take them out. Are you still walking when you should have been taken out? Are you still showing up at work when you know the boss really does not want you? Are you still in your right mind yet you keep on walking in the midst of your fire?

Shadrach, Meshech, and Abednego got thrown into the fire, bound, but now, they're walking. How do you go in bound and then walk in what was supposed to take you out? God did not use the fire to burn them, but to burn up what tied them up. Only God can use the stuff that was supposed to burn you up to set you free. Have you been set free by what was supposed to take you out?

The Hebrew boys are walking around in the fire,

Nebuchadnezzar looks in and said, "hey, how many did we throw in there?" Three. Well, who is the other one looking like God? That is the thing, He is God. When you see me walking through bad situations, it's not just me walking through it; I have Somebody walking with me Who is bigger than my situation.

So, they're walking around, and Nebuchadnezzar comes near the door, but not too near, because this is the same furnace that burned up his own people. First, he ordered them to be thrown in, now he asks them to come out. The text says though they had been thrown in, they walked out. That is God's Word to you. You got thrown in a bad situation, but God is right there with you and He will give you power to walk out. Then, the text says that their consequences could not be explained or contained by their circumstances. Everybody started to examine them: no hair singed, no clothes burned. You were in a fire, but you didn't burn up! You were in a fire, but there are no fifth degree burns. Your consequences can't be explained or contained by your circumstances. Shadrach, Meshech, and Abednego had been in the fire, but they didn't look like they had been in a fire. A whole lot of people have been to hell and back, but you couldn't tell. A whole lot of people have been through the fire, but they don't look like it. A lot of people have been heart-broken, but they don't look like it.

III. GOD WILL USE WHAT YOU HAVE BEEN THROUGH TO SET THE STAGE

FOR A PROMOTION FOR YOU

Finally, **God will use what you have been through to set the stage for a promotion for you.** The text says that Shadrach, Meshech, and Abednego got promoted in the place that was supposed to take them out. If you look back over your life, you may be doing well right now, but look at what God did. God didn't take you out of that situation, He gave you a promotion in that situation.

The boys got promoted, but faith was what got them there. We can turn this thing right if we do it by faith, have standards that we stand on, and a faith that releases God to show up and show out, knowing God will use this horrible time in the life of our community as a promotion, where we, as a community recognize that oppressive lyrics do not belong in our music. We will support good rap, we will support holy hip-hop, and we will support that which is healthy, and define it appropriately.

Here's the deal: I've discovered that sometimes before you get to, you've got to go through. A lot of us want to get to certain things and places, but you can't just get there automatically; you have to go through.

The first time I went to the Caribbean, I went to Jamaica. I had a wonderful time, but when my plane landed, my bags were not with me. I was at the baggage claim and I didn't see my bags. I immediately went to the baggage area and I went ballistic. I said, "Listen, where are my bags?" I was complaining, complaining, and complaining. The person at the counter got on the computer, and then said, "Oh sir, your baggage came in with an earlier flight. You're at the wrong window. You're at the 'complaint' window. You need to go to 'claims' to get what you are looking for."

A whole lot of us spend too much time at the "complaint" window when God says you need to go to "claims" to get what you are looking for. So, I asked, "Where is claims?" They said, "Oh, it's not in this building; it's in the building down the block." So I said, "Okay, but I just heard thunder and I just saw lightning, rain is coming down." And he said, "Well, if you want to get to claims, you've got to go through the rain."

Do you know that God has something better for you? If God has it better for you, you are going to have to go through the storm. But I promise you if you keep your head through the storm, you do not have to go by yourself. He will walk with you. He will talk with you. He will see you through if you don't bow to the wrong music.

WHAT'S UP WITH THE DOWN-LOW?

Now there was a man of the Pharisees named Nicodemus, a member of the Jewish ruling council. He came to Jesus at night and said, "Rabbi, we know you are a teacher who has come from God. For no one could perform the miraculous signs you are doing if God were not with him."

In reply Jesus declared, "I tell you the truth, no one can see the kingdom of God unless he is born again." "How can a man be born when he is old?" Nicodemus asked. "Surely he cannot enter a second time into his mother's womb to be born!"

Jesus answered, "I tell you the truth, no one can enter the kingdom of God unless he is born of water and the Spirit. Flesh gives birth to flesh, but the Spirit gives birth to spirit. You should not be surprised at my saying, 'You must be born again.' The wind blows wherever it pleases. You hear its sound, but you cannot tell where it comes from or where it is going. So it is with everyone born of the Spirit."

—John 3:1-8

Nicodemus, a ruler of the Jews, a member of the Pharisees,

came to Jesus at night. Jesus, in essence, said to him, **"Ye shall know the truth and the truth shall set you free."**

If one is living a lie, he is walking as a prisoner without bars. Whenever you are living a lie, you are locked up from the inside out. You have been sentenced to a prison of guilt, insecurity, and yes, even fear. Then you discover the reality—the truth. I believe it was Ernest T. Campbell, who wrote the book titled *Locked in a Room with Open Doors.* I hang out here, homiletically, because I am convinced that regardless of your lifestyle or orientation, if you are living a lie, if what you are on the inside is contradicted by what you do on the outside, you are locked up from the inside out. If you are leading a double life, where some people see you one way, but other people see you in a completely different way, you are *locked in a room with open doors;* you are locked up from the inside out.

I deal with this particular subject matter because I am concerned that in the African-American community there is a segment of our male population that is leading and living a life that is a lie. In other words, they are living on the "down-low."

Permit me to share with you a few case studies. Some of these studies I am familiar with because the people involved have shared their experiences with me; others I have read about.

The first story is about a man by the name of Hank, (whose name I have changed to protect other persons involved in this story). Hank, at one point in his life, was the embodiment of success. In spite of racism in these yet to be United States of America, Hank was able to climb the ladder of success. As a matter of fact, Hank had all of the signs of success and achievement. There were others who were envious of him because he, seemingly, had it going on. He was married to a gorgeous sister; he was handsome himself; he was sophisticated, cultivated, and educated. On top of that, he and his wife had two beautiful children.

Privately, Hank was, in his own words, being, "pushed and pulled by some ugly urges and diabolical desires." Hank found himself over and over again attracted to and fantasizing about men. To make matters worse, in the course of intimacy with his wife, in order to be turned on and stay turned on, he fantasized about men. Hank, on the outside appeared to have it going on, but Hank, on the inside, according to his own words, was being "pushed and pulled by ugly urges and diabolical desires."

Isn't it true, that in too many instances, we often judge people by what we see on the outside, and yet we have no clue as to the hell they are catching on the inside? I love what our old saints used to say: "There is so much bad in the best of us and so much good in the worst of us, it really doesn't behoove any of us to talk about the rest of us." So, be careful about judging someone based on what you see, because oftentimes it's the stuff that you can't see that is defining and determining who they are, what they are about, and what is really going on with them.

So, Hank was being driven by these "ugly urges and diabolical desires" which he could control. One day, Hank accepted an offer to go to lunch with one of the men he had been eyeing, thinking that no one saw him eyeing this man. Well, lunch led to dinner, dinner led to something else, one thing led to another. Now imagine how Hank must have felt as he went home every night to a wonderful woman and beautiful children, but he is living on the "down-low."

Hank was a faithful member of a church, and also served on the deacon board. Imagine how he must have felt as he heard sermons by preachers talking about how heinous it is to be a homosexual. Hank heard sermons about what an abomination to Almighty God it is to be a homosexual. He was not about to come out of the closet though, and admit his own "ugly urges." Why? Because he would hear sermons that would down him and diss him and make him feel even more uncomfortable with what he had become and what he was doing.

Not only is there Hank, but there is Timothy. Now, Timothy is another story all together, because Timothy was raped as a child by his uncle. Being raped as a child by his own uncle, Timothy began, as I shared with you earlier about Marvin Gaye, to doubt his own sexuality. To make matters worse, he was very effeminate in his characteristics. So, imagine how Timothy must have felt as he wrestled with his own issues. But again, Timothy did not want to be seen, especially in a black culture, as a homosexual. What did Timothy do? He got married. But he had never really processed or recovered from the pain of being raped as a child, and consequently, Timothy found himself also slipping at night into other dark relationships.

Not only is there Hank and Timothy, but there is also Ricky. Now, Ricky was a preacher of the Gospel of Jesus Christ, and he wasn't about to go to church and come clean about his chosen lifestyle. After all, he had a wonderful wife, and he had not two, but five kids. Consequently, Ricky found himself overcompensating for his own issues, by always preaching in a very down and judgmental way about homosexuality. He even ran a revival at his church and blasted homosexuals. Imagine how all of these men must have felt, caught in a web of darkness and negativity about their own sense of identity.

It is very few of us who do not identify in an up-close and personal fashion with the reality that there might be one person we know who is engaging in what we perceive to be deviant sexual behavior.

J. Lynn Harris came out with his book that dealt with the "down-low." Then another brother wrote another book talking about the "down-low"—a journey into the lives of straight men who sleep with men, not gay men who sleep with men, but straight men who sleep with men.

Here is what this other brother said as he is being interviewed. He justifies his own disposition as it relates to his identity. He said, "I refuse to let you label me, because if you label me that means I will live down to the label that you have for me. I'm not going out like that." He defiantly continued, "Really it's just about sex for me. So, I'm not gay. I'm just someone who likes sex with men. Yes, I'm married. Yes, I have a wife. But, I'm not living a lie; I have just lied to her about my sex. I still love her. I still care about her."

Imagine that! This is a brother who calls himself straight, yet he sleeps with other men. This is how they came up with the term "on the down-low" or "on the D.L." Now, what exactly is the "down-low"? The "down-low" is simply a brother who is living a double life of sexuality, under the cover of darkness and deceit, where he sleeps with other men, but he does not call himself gay or bisexual.

The unfortunate thing is, in this nation, black males have always had their sexuality criminalized and demonized. You may be familiar with the book or the movie, *To Kill a Mockingbird*. It's the story of a brother whose sexuality is demonized by the white power structure. Understand that from the time we were kidnapped and brought here as slaves, white folk have demonized and criminalized black males' sexuality. There is dysfunctionality in the African-

American community because we have not dealt with how we were demonized and criminalized. It was seen in so many instances during slavery—a brother was emasculated as he helplessly watched his woman being raped by the master. That is a part of the criminalization of our sexuality. On the other hand, the one thing that the white male did not want was for the big black male brute to get involved, sexually, with their pure, chaste white women. This is called the criminalization and demonization of black male sexuality.

There is still a fear on the part of some white men whenever they see a black man with a white woman. As a matter of fact, if you recall, in the late '90s, a brother in Atlanta had engaged in consensual sex with a white girl, and was sentenced to life in prison. Why? Because there is still a mentality in this country that demonizes and criminalizes black male sexuality. So, on the one hand, you have oppression at work, on the other hand, you have the internalization of that oppression. As one writer puts it: "This is the pedagogue of the oppressed where black folk have internalized the oppression of the enemy." Having internalizing that oppression, we do not process what has happened to us, and when you don't process what happens to you, it gets in you; and when it gets in you, you begin to act out what is in you because you have not adequately dealt with and healed from what happened.

Understand that when we talk about the "down-low" it has to do with straight men who engage in homosexual activity, but yet they maintain their relationship with women. The sad thing is, they are living a lie. It's a culture of deceit. What bothers me is that the black church has become complicit in this culture of deceit. The one place you don't talk about sex is in the black church. The one place you don't deal with all of the ramifications and realities of sex is in the black church.

Then there are some of us—the last thing we want to deal with is talking to our kids about sex, even though they're watching BET and MTV, and all of these X-rated videos. We don't talk to our kids about sex, and the thing that blows my mind is that you were created by God, and God, in His creativity, decided to use an act of sex to bring you into the world. If we don't have proper sex education, we will not live a life of liberation. Only when we allow our spirituality to shape our sexuality can we fulfill our possibilities and reach our sacred destiny.

So, we have this "down-low" phenomenon going on. The church is complaisant because they don't talk about sex. Then, to make matters worse, when we do talk about sex, we talk in such a judgmental, hateful fashion, so much so that a lot of brothers feel pushed into a dark corner and cannot admit that living this lifestyle is not acceptable in the church. Why? Because we have a bunch of adulterers who will look down their sanctimonious noses at them and say, how dare you do that? Yet these same people are sleeping with everybody except their wives.

We have become hypocritical in the church when it comes to actually discussing, teaching, and dealing with the idea of homosexuality. Consequently, the black church has often been guilty of homophobia, in that we hate homosexuals even though we have pews that are populated by them. They have gone underground, and they are in the dark, on the "down-low," because of the complaisant attitude of the church of Jesus Christ. I serve a God Who sets us free, so you do not have to live another day on the "down-low" because that is "low-down." God wants you to be who God made you to be; live as God made you and as God defined you.

Based on the Scripture passage at the beginning of this chapter, some of you might be thinking: was Nicodemus gay? Nicodemus was not gay. He was a Pharisee, a ruler of the Jews, a man whose social orientation contradicted him hooking up with Jesus.

There is a whole lot of talk and dialogue right now about whether or not homosexuals choose this lifestyle or whether or not they were born this way. Scientists have even decided through studies, and have come up with the fact that there are both animals and humans who are predisposed by way of their genetic makeup to becoming homosexuals, meaning they are born that way.

I'm not wrestling with that right now, but what I am dealing with is this—Nicodemus' social orientation was not to be seen with Jesus. Nicodemus was a Pharisee.

Pharisees hated Jesus. Nicodemus was a ruler of the Jews. The Jews had already declared war on Jesus. The Book says, under the cover of night, Nicodemus went to see Jesus. Jesus said to Nicodemus, "you are coming to me on the 'down-low,' but, I'm about to blow you away in such an awesome way with the Truth of the Gospel, that you're not going to leave Me the same way you came. You came on the 'down-low,' but after you leave Me, you will be delivered."

Pastor Jeffrey Johnson told this story, (and I had a similar experience when I was in Washington D.C.). Anyway, we were blown away because when we turned a corner, there in the middle of the street was a bed. There was a traffic jam because of that bed being in the middle of the street. Accidents were created because of that bed being in the wrong place. Pastor Jeffrey Johnson said, "You always know your bed is in the wrong place whenever there is too much traffic in your bed."

This "down-low" thing has placed some beds in the wrong places. We've had women get wounded because the bed was in the wrong place. Children are confused because the bed was in the wrong place. Is there hope and help? Is there peace, power, and a prescription for those whose bed is in the wrong place? Yes, there is. Do you want to know how it works? Let me give you three points:

I. ONLY GOD CAN USE THE NIGHT

TO HELP YOU SEE THE LIGHT

Only God can use the night to help you see the light.
Only God can use the dark to help you see what you would
not have seen had it not gone dark in your life. Dr. King
put it this way: "Only when it is dark enough can you see
the stars." Here's what is killing me about this text. The
text says that Nicodemus came to Jesus at night, and
because he came to Jesus at night, Jesus helped him to see
the light.

I'm reading this powerful series of slave narratives, and
the more I read about our slave mothers and fathers, the
more I have an appreciation for the amazing strength that
they had, and the fact that that strength is in our DNA.
Whenever you feel like you can't handle whatever you're
going through, I dare you to read our slave narratives,
and remember the hell our parents lived in every single
day. They did not have access to counseling; all they had
was prayer. They did not have access to medication; all
they had was the Lord of their liberation and salvation.

Anyway, I was reading this one particular narrative about
this brother who ran away in 1863. The brother found
himself hiding in a barn one night. He testifies like this,
"I was hiding in the barn when suddenly the darkness
was broken by light from a lantern. I'm afraid because the
dark was going to be my cover, the dark was going to
keep me safe. And now, all of a sudden, light breaks the
darkness, and I know I'm no longer safe because I was

counting on the dark to keep me safe, but while I was in the dark, the one who came in there with the lantern, heard some movement, came where I was, and told me the good news that Abe Lincoln had signed the Emancipation Proclamation. And that's when I came up out of my hiding place; I came to receive the light of my freedom."

You may not be where you should be because you are still walking in darkness. But God, in His grace, can come to you in the darkness of your situation, and bring you to the light.

Here's the interesting thing—the brother testifies that when the lantern first broke the darkness, he had to cover his eyes because the light hurt. Truth is light. Whenever you are sharing and teaching truth, some people can't handle it. Truth as light breaks in on the darkness they have been used to and some folk have enjoyed the darkness so long that their whole testimony is: "don't confuse me with the facts, my mind is already made up."

So Nicodemus said, "Jesus, here's the deal: you are a bad Man. Matter of fact, You have to come from God because nobody can do the stuff You do unless the Lord is with them." Jesus doesn't even bother to bask in the compliment, but said, "Nicodemus, here's the deal. I tell you the truth, no one can see the Kingdom of God unless he's born again. You've come to Me under the cover of darkness, on the 'down-low.' Here is the light: your past does not define your possibilities."

II. I WAS BORN THIS WAY AS OPPOSED TO, I CHOSE THIS WAY

Now, I'm about to get in trouble with some folks, because these men, living on the "down-low," argue over orientation—**"I was born this way,"** **as opposed to "I chose this way."** Jesus said, "regardless of how you were born, you were all born in sin and shapened in iniquity," and, "Nicodemus, I know this is going contrary to everything you've been taught to believe." What have you been taught to believe? That you are a product of your past, that who you are is a direct result of all you've been through and where you have been. Jesus said, "no, that isn't how life is. Since I'm here now the deal is this: I don't care where you've been or what you've been through, you can be born again; and when you're born again it means your past does not determine your possibilities."

"You must be born again." That is the light under the cover of night. Nicodemus said, "okay, Lord, do you mean I have to go back to mama's womb to be born?" Jesus replied, "Nicodemus, you're smarter than that. You have an education. You can't put toothpaste back in the tube and you can't go back into your mama's womb. So, I'm going to radically redefine your theology that will redemptively reshape and redefine your anthropology which will now govern your biology: Nicodemus, **'that which is born of flesh is flesh, but that which is born of spirit is spirit.'** 'You must be born again.'"

Dr. Michael Eric Dyson put it this way: "Your sexuality when it's defined by your spirituality means that you are pursuing your sexuality in the context of your relationship with Almighty God." So, when God starts to define your sexuality, anything that is dysfunctional and deviant because of your past is no longer the predominating factor in your life. Why? Because now you are operating, not with your biology defining your anthropology, but your psychology has been fed by your theology, and your theology has defined your anthropology, and your anthropology defined by your theology gives you a new sense of biology.

III. THERE IS NO TELLING WHAT THE HOLY GHOST CAN DO FOR YOU

There is no telling what the Holy Ghost can do for you. The text says the wind blows where it wants to blow— you hear it, but you don't know where it came from, and you don't know where it's going, because the wind has what Dr. Manuel Scott called "an unlimited freedom." The wind can blow wherever it pleases and so that means you can't tell who can get saved; you can't tell what a person cannot become. God deliver me from hypocritical, judgmental, sanctimonious Christians who want to tell somebody, because of their sexual orientation, whether or not they can be saved. The wind blows where it wants to blow.

Dr. Scott has an awesome sermon about this. In the sermon, he said he grew up in Waco, Texas, and in Waco there was deep segregation—white folk didn't let black folk go to certain places in town. But Dr. Scott says the one thing white folk could not control was where the wind blew. He says the wind that blew on their side of town would blow on his side of town. Don't you ever tell anybody what they can't become, because once the wind of the Spirit starts to blow, it can save me, it can save you, and it can save anybody.

The wind has such power that even though you can't see it, you can always see its effects. All I am is a living effect of the wind. Every time I stand up and preach, it isn't me preaching, it's the wind blowing. I go to my pulpit some Sundays, just knowing I am going to throw down, and I flunk big time. I go there other Sundays, just knowing I am going to die, but somehow the Word goes forth, folk get saved, lives get changed, and I'm trying to figure it out. Are you honest enough to testify that there is some stuff in your life that really was just a bunch of nothing, but once the wind got a hold of it, the next thing you knew, it took you places you never thought you would go?

One February there was a terrible windstorm that blew through Dallas. I was driving by our old church site where we used to be off of Kiest Blvd. I just like to go by there every now and then because it keeps me grounded in God. I would drive to our old church site, sit there, and look at where we began. And I'll start thanking God because now we are in a bigger church facility and the pyramid on top of our new building is bigger than the entire church we used to have off of Kiest Blvd. All I can do is thank God because the wind took us to where we are now.

Anyway, I was just sitting out there and looking at the little garden out front one day. All of a sudden, I saw this card blowing in the wind. I followed it because it had blown a long way from the Shell station at the corner of Kiest Blvd. and Hwy 67. It had been in a trash bin, but the wind had opened up the trash bin and had blown the card out of the bin. So, I got out of my car and went to pick it up, and I discovered it was a note card. I still have that card because the message on the front of it said:

> *To someone special:*
> *You are God's miracle.*
> *Don't give up.*
> *Love,*
> *So-n-So.*

The message on the card began to talk to my heart. It said, Freddy, that is my testimony. Somebody threw me away, somebody gave up on me, but the message I have is, even though they threw me away, God's wind blew where I was and it took me out of the trash.

Have you been trashed? Have you been thrown away, but God rescued you out of that bad situation? Have you been lifted from your "down-low" lifestyle by the love of Jesus Christ? No matter what your situation is, God is saying to you, ***you must be born again.*** God will bring you from your "down-low" lifestyle to an up-higher lifestyle. Let the wind blow you into your true destiny.

AREN'T YOU
SICK OF THIS?

Some time later, Jesus went up to Jerusalem for a feast of the Jews. Now there is in Jerusalem near the Sheep Gate a pool, which in Aramaic is called Bethesda and which is surrounded by five covered colonnades. Here a great number of disabled people used to lie—the blind, the lame, the paralyzed. One who was there had been an invalid for thirty-eight years. When Jesus saw him lying there and learned that he had been in this condition for a long time, he asked him, "Do you want to get well?"

"Sir," the invalid replied, "I have no one to help me into the pool when the water is stirred. While I am trying to get in, someone else goes down ahead of me."

Then Jesus said to him, "Get up! Pick up your mat and walk." At once the man was cured; he picked up his mat and walked. The day on which this took place was a Sabbath.

—John 5:1-9

Later Jesus found him at the temple and said to him, "See, you are well again. Stop sinning or something worse may happen to you."

—John 5:14

Who do you think you are? Whose are you that informs who you think you are? What do you believe about the God above Who informs and inspires how you view yourself? Does your theology inform and instruct your psychology so much so that it gives you an appropriate anthropology that dictates your biology, so that, in a real sense, you have a healthy sociology?

I raise these questions because I have discovered that, sadly and sinfully, religion that is repressive and oppressive has a way of dividing the body from the soul. And whenever you divide the body from the soul, you justify doing anything with the body, as long as the soul is saved. Whenever you divide the body from the soul, you soon become politically ineffective, socially irrelevant, and economically inept. Why? Because you place so much emphasis on the soul that you have no problem whatsoever neglecting what is going on with the body. That is a twisted theology that is rooted in a Eurocentric Greek Americanity as opposed to Afro-Asiatic Christianity.

If we are not careful, we will be put into a religion that was used to repress and oppress us, by dividing the body from the soul. Understand that the Europeans who engaged in the trans-Atlantic slave trade called themselves Christians. These same Christians who were responsible for colonialism in Africa and apartheid in South Africa, exported a religion that divided the body from the soul. After all, when this nation was formed, the Europeans looked for some way to justify the oppression of Africans who had been kidnapped and who somehow survived the heinous horrors of the Middle Passage. They were treated not as persons to be respected, but as property to be misused. The Europeans mistreated and dehumanized us, to the point of labeling us three-fifths of a human being.

The same constitution that eloquently espouses that "we hold these truths to be self-evident that all men are created equal," at the same time, with a double standard, describes us as three-fifths of a human being. They further began to comfort their conscience by simply saying, "if we are going to avoid going to hell ourselves, we must do something to save these savages." Understand, their mindset was that we were less than human, and yet we had souls. So because in their warped theology there was a division between body and soul, they said, "we don't mind their bodies catching hell, as long as their souls go to Heaven when they die. They can experience an existential hell down here, but if we save their souls, at least they will spend eternity in the presence of Jesus Christ."

What a twisted theology! What a sick sociology! What an abominable anthropology! It's a theology that divides the body from the soul. It's a theology that says, as long as the soul is saved, it does not matter what we do to the body.

The sad thing is, in the pedagogy of the oppressed, we soon learn that those who are oppressed are guilty of internalizing the oppression that they have been subjected to. Just as a boat with a leak allows what is around it to get in it and causes it to sink, those who are oppressed, in too many instances, allow what has happened to them to get in them. They so internalize it, that it begins to sink them.

I'm dealing with this because sadly, there are many of us who have unwittingly adopted this twisted theology that divides the body from the soul. This twisted theology is Eurocentric, in that, it is rooted in a Greek version of Americanity, and not Afro-Asiatic Christianity. How do I know?

When you read the Genesis account of Creation, understand the Bible says that when God created humanity, He formed us out of the dust of the earth. And then the Bible says that God breathed into the nostrils of man, and man became a living soul. Man *became* a living soul, simply means: I do not have a soul, I am a soul. The Hebrew word for *soul* is *nephesh*. And the word *nephesh* simply refers to all that we are; it does not divide the body from the soul. But, it says that the body and the soul are one, and they are animated and liberated by the invigorating activity of God's Holy Spirit. My prayer is that we would stop dividing our bodies from our souls.

You may get upset when you go to church, and the

preacher has the unmitigated gall to talk about politics and the economic-social condition in which we find ourselves. We don't mind the preacher preaching to us about how to handle our situation, but we don't want the preacher to deal with the injustice in that situation. Sadly, there are so many folks who come to my church, and they tune me out, because they have divided the body from the soul. All they want is to hear about what will feed their soul, but that is contrary to the meaning of Scripture which says, "I am a living soul." That means wherever I go, I'm a soul; on my job, I'm a soul; in the community, I'm a soul; at home, I'm a soul. So, don't divide my body from my soul because I'm concerned about my body because my body is a reflection of what is on the inside. The bottom line is, I am a living, breathing soul.

Still, we like to divide the body from the soul, and when we divide the body from the soul, we will overlook the harsh reality of what came down at the Supreme Court a while back—led by someone who looks like us, but always is against us, who had the audacity to issue a verdict that has set this nation back sixty years. The man who inherited the mantle of Thurgood Marshall is guilty of spitting on the sacrifices and blood of Thurgood Marshall. I know some of you were saying, "well, really I don't mind not busing my kids across town." The issue isn't about busing; the issue has to do with the different ways we fund public education in this nation. The sad thing is, this nation has a discriminatory and different way of funding public education. It isn't about me sitting in a classroom with somebody white; it's about me having the same access to resources as those who live in other sections that are richer in this nation.

I don't divide my body from my soul because if I divide my body from my soul I allow you to make me content with just taking my soul to Heaven after I die, instead of dealing with the harsh realities that my soul must deal with on this earth, before I die. God, deliver us from a religion that is myopic where we divide the body from the soul because it is contrary to the Word of God. And whenever we do that, we even begin to mistreat, disrespect, and neglect our own bodies, because our thing is, as long as our souls are happy, it doesn't matter how we treat our bodies.

I'm about to get in trouble right now because I'm a black preacher talking to black people about their bodies. I'm a black preacher talking to black people about how they handle their physicalities. Many times, we don't mind talking about our spirituality, but don't you talk about what I feed my body. Don't you bring me to church and talk to me about my lack of exercising, or about the fact that I cannot feed my live body dead food, and not expect to have a dead end. Don't you talk to me about my body; just talk to me about my soul. I am talking about your soul!

We black folk are the most religious folk on the planet—

we pray longer, we stay in church longer, we sing louder, and we preach harder; but physically, we are the most unhealthy folk on the face of the planet.

We are at the top of every negative statistic about health—when it comes to AIDS, diabetes, hypertension, heart disease, cancer—we are at the front of it all. Aren't we the same folk who pray Sunday after Sunday? Aren't we the same folk who go to church more than anybody else? Yet, we're the sickest people out there. We are overweight, and undernourished. We are suffering from obesity. We are suffering from high blood pressure and sugar and all of the cancers out there, but our souls are happy because we are on our way to Heaven, anyhow.

The Bible says: **Present your bodies a living sacrifice, holy and acceptable unto God which is your spiritual service of worship** (Romans 12:1).

Jesus said: **I have come that you might have life and have it more abundantly** (John 10:10).

The Bible says: **Don't you know you are the temple of the Holy Spirit?** (2 Corinthians 6:16)

If you went to your church facility on a given Sunday, and it was torn up, broken down, messed up, trashed up, and dirty, you would be talking about the pastor and the staff saying, "they are just so sorry; they can't even keep God's House clean. They are messing up God's House." I don't know if you've read the Bible lately, but the Bible says in the Old Testament, God had a House that was called the Temple. It was made of physical materials. But in the New Testament, since Jesus has come, Jesus says, you ought to look at the Temple of God, which is your body. If your body is broken down, if you are overweight and obese, if you are suffering from high blood pressure, how can you truly be the temple of God's Holy Spirit?

I'm talking about your physical body. You don't walk. You don't exercise. You don't eat right. The late comedian, Robin Harris, put it like this: "Black folk, we got a wait problem. We can't wait to eat." And we don't care what it is we eat, as long as it tastes good and it's good to us. I got to have ham hock because the ham hock is what seasons my greens real good, and the greasier the better. The more lard you put in there, the better off you are, in terms of how it tastes. We have justified neglecting our bodies by dividing our bodies from our souls, and that is an unbiblical theology that comes from an oppressive religion that was handed down to us by those who wanted to keep us down.

The Bible says that Jesus, Heaven's Hero and Earth's Emancipator, comes to Jerusalem during a high and holy season, and He purposely goes to an area that was populated by those who were pathetic and pitiful. It is a holding area for those who were hopeless and helpless. Look at the sadness of it—these are blind folk and lame folk, and they are positioned near the pool. Isn't that where black folk are now? We are positioned near the pool.

I told you earlier how *USA Today* did a series of articles on the fact that where you live has a lot to do with how long you live. Why? Because there are areas in this nation that are downright unhealthy. I hope you'll go to see Michael Moore's latest movie/documentary called *Sicko*, in which he deals with the sick healthcare system in these yet to be United States of America.

Please understand this—black folk are being burdened and broken by the terrible healthcare system; it's not even a healthcare system, it's a medical care system. It is a system that is based on profit. It is a system where the pharmaceutical companies are more concerned with dollars than they are with deliverance. So, as a consequence, we live in a nation that has a broken healthcare system that benefits those who own the system. Why do you think this administration, in the face of almost fifty million Americans without healthcare, has never talked about universal healthcare? Because if we had universal healthcare, it would cut into the pocket of many of those who benefit from this sick system.

This is one of the things that we need to be aware of. We, as a people, are at the pool, and all of our dysfunctionality is at the pool with us. I want you to see us at the pool; see us at the pool with sickle cell disease; see us at the pool with HIV/AIDS killing more black women between the ages of eighteen and thirty-four than any other community. See us at the pool! Until we recognize that our bodies are not disconnected from our souls, until we get a new theology that realizes that God wants us to recognize our bodies as temples of God's Holy Spirit, we are going to stay at the pool. But, Jesus comes to bring our body and our soul back together.

Dr. Zan Wesley Holmes, Jr., said that once he went to a symphony to hear a great orchestra play, and while he was sitting in the balcony with his father, he was blown away because at first there was all of this discordant music being played. It is like everybody on stage was playing whatever they wanted to play. Then suddenly, the conductor walked in and stood behind the podium. The conductor then raised his baton, and guess what? Everything went silent. Then the conductor brought the baton down, and suddenly what was discordant music turned into concordant music, what was a cacophony became a symphony. Why? Because everything that was going in different directions was brought together when they followed the direction of the conductor.

You have divided your life up—body from soul—the Conductor has just walked in; the Conductor is waving His baton, and wants to bring your life back together, so your life can make the music that God wants it to make.

How do we do it? Let me give you three important points:

I. Jesus Sets Us Free from the Inside Out

The text lets us know that **Jesus sets us free from the inside out**—He sets us free from those prisons that have become our comfort zones. If you are not careful, you will become comfortable in that which has incarcerated you.

Some folk have been down so long that being down does not bother them. Some folk have learned to function so well in their dysfunctionality that if you dare take them out of their dysfunctionality, they will get mad at you. Some folk have been down so long and dysfunctional so long that they are just like those Hebrew slaves that God used Moses to set free, and once they were set free, they kept saying, "at least back in Egypt, we had slave food and a place to die."

The sad thing is, we have allowed, by our division of the body and soul, the church to become a glorified casket where we join the church as a place to have our funeral. We say to ourselves, "when I get sick, I have somebody to come visit me, and pray for me." Well, I am not pastoring my church just to make sure people have a good funeral or have someone visit them in the hospital; I am pastoring my church because I want somebody to have a healthy life, I want somebody to lead a fruitful life, I want somebody not just to live long, but to live well.

So, Jesus goes up to the man and says, "Do you want to be well?" This really messed with me because this man had been sick for thirty-eight years, and strangely Jesus asked him, "Do you want to be well?" Now, if I had been sick for thirty-eight years, I know I would not have wanted to stay in that condition.

It dawned on me that some folk really don't want to be well. Some folk would rather stay in their sick situation because they are used to being sick. As a matter of fact, some folk have learned to nurture their sickness because the more they nurture their sickness, the more attention they get. The more they have a pity-party for their pathetic predicament, the more attention they get. They feel some folk won't pay them attention unless they are sick.

Once I went to the hospital to visit someone, and sitting outside the door was someone with an oxygen tank, smoking. I just could not ignore this situation, and I wanted to ask this person, do you want to be well, or do you enjoy being sick? But, instead, as I was passing by, I just said, "I am really praying for you." That person recognized me, and then she had the nerve to say, "Pastor, I listen to you every day on K104." I said, "Look, I'm praying for you that the next time I come here, number one, you are not here, and number two, you do not have that cigarette in your hand. That cigarette is going to kill you." Do you know what she said back to me? She said, "It's going to kill me if I don't have this cigarette."

What kind of sickness is it that has such a hold on a person that they hold on to that which is responsible for them being sick in the first place? And before you think I am just talking about folks who smoke, I am also talking to those who act as though they can't get enough bacon and can't get enough ribs. I'm asking you the same question that Jesus asked the man at the pool, "Do you want to get well?"

If you do, please do this—Take that thing of bacon or that slab of pork ribs that you have, put it on your windowsill and just leave it for several days. Within five days or less, you will see all kinds of maggots and worms coming out of that meat. The same maggots and worms you see on that windowsill, coming out of that meat, is what will be living in your behind by the time you get through eating all of that pork. Let's go on.

II. Your Excuses will Always get in the Way and Leave you Thinking Everybody Else is Responsible for Your Being in the Situation that You are In

Jesus asked the man, "Do you want to be well?" Notice that the man comes up with a couple of excuses. He does not even answer the question. He says, "Sir, I would have been well by now, but I do not have anybody to help me.

Every time I try to roll over, somebody jumps in ahead of me."

Now, first of all, let me deal with his excuses. The sad thing is, **your excuses will always get in the way and leave you thinking everybody else is responsible for your being in the situation that you are in**. If this man's problem was getting into the water, then what he should have been doing is inching his behind along, at least making some progress toward the edge of the pool, so the next time the water stirred, he could fall over into it. You do not have any excuse. For many of us reading this book, our paralysis isn't physical, it's psychological. Some of us need to understand our sickness. That is why in the medical profession they talk about psychosomatic illness, which basically deals with the fact that some sicknesses start in our heads and manifest themselves in our bodies because there is no disconnect between the soul and the body.

Notice he has all these excuses, but Jesus says, "all right, you know what? I'm tired of your excuses. Rise, take up your bed. Walk." After Jesus sets us free from the inside out by dealing with what's on our minds that will often confuse us, Jesus says, "rise, you've been waiting on the water to stir. I am the Living Water."

Our mothers and fathers didn't go to seminary, but they had a theology that they lived by every day. They didn't have an education, but God gave them revelation. They had a hermeneutic on this passage that messes me up. They used to sing: "Wade in the water, wade in the water, children, God's gonna trouble the water." That was based on John chapter five, according to educator and theologian, Dr. Howard Thurman. We often use it now in the context of baptism, but that was not the context they used it in back then. They used it in the context of slavery, where this passage lets them know when you wade in the water, after God troubles the water, on the other side of that trouble is healing.

When they would escape to freedom up North, after leaving the plantation, in order to make sure the hound dogs were thrown off of their scent, they would wade in the water. They knew once they reached the other side of the water that there was freedom, and so they sang, "Wade in the water because God's gonna trouble the water." Only God can use the trouble that you go through to set you free on the other side. Are you where you are today because God used trouble as your transportation?

I know I am where I am today, not because I made the best choices, not because my life has been smooth, but because every now and then, God troubled the waters, and God said what's behind me isn't going to catch up with me, and once I reach the other side, I will be free. Rise! Grab your bed! Get to steppin'! Once Jesus gets in your life, He liberates you from "can't" so you begin to live in the power of "can."

III. If you Allow the Word to Get in You and Stay in You, You Can't Stay the Same Way You Are

Have you ever been in a situation that was so rough and you knew you didn't have what it took to handle it? Jesus is telling you to rise. Take up your bed. Get to stepping. Walk it out. Walk! The Bible says at that moment, the man got up and walked. Where did he get it from? He got it from the power of Jesus' words. When the Word that was spoken to him got in him, it made a difference for him. I promise you, **if you allow the Word to get in you and stay in you, you can't stay the same way you are.** If the Word really gets in you, your faith gets stronger, and your prayer life gets better.

Have you heard about that young college student who was driving somewhere? Momma let him use her car, and after driving for a while, he got lost. So he got out of the car to go get some directions. As soon as he got out of the car, he threw the key up and tried to catch it, but the key went down into a sewer hole. So he got on the cell phone, called his Mother, and said, "Momma, I'm sorry, I'm lost, and to make matters worse I lost the key to the car. What do I do, Momma?" Momma said, "Son, didn't you see that Bible I left, on purpose, in the passenger seat? This is your first time driving my car by yourself, and so I wasn't taking any chances. I had God's Word right there with you." He said, "Momma, I don't have time to have church. I need to know what I'm supposed to do now because I am lost and I don't have a key to get the car started; it's down in the sewer hole." Momma said, "Well, evidently, you have not read the Word. I always keep a spare key to the car in the Bible so all you got to do is open up the Bible and you will discover your key is in the Word." This young college student got home safely because he discovered the key in the Word. Do you know your key is in the Word?

The lame man got up and walked. The Bible says, he is walking with his bed—the bed that used to carry him, he is now carrying. As he is walking with the bed, some pious haters say to him, "this is Sabbath, what are you doing carrying your bed on the Sabbath?" Now, you know they are haters because they are not congratulating him on the fact that he was down all these years and now he's up. They are so pious that all they care about is keeping rules.

You have some church folk in the 21st Century who have no concern about the fact that somebody who was once a hoochie is now going to church; they are concerned that she still dresses like a hoochie. Don't you know you can't clean a fish you haven't caught yet? You haven't always dressed all holy yourself. You haven't always had a handkerchief over your legs. You used to uncross your legs and say, "come and get it."

The Bible says they said, "who told you to carry this bed?" He said, "the Man who told me to rise, take up my bed, and walk." Later, Jesus saw him and said, "don't get into any more sin, or what happened to you thirty-eight years ago may get worse."

Evidently, he made a spiritual choice that had some physical consequences. He did something back then that was crippling him for thirty-eight years. Some of you did something way back then and it has had crippling consequences ever since then. There is no dichotomy between the body and the soul. And so, what He is saying here is, "I'm giving you another chance so you can make another choice. I'm giving you another chance, when everybody else had given up on you, when everybody else thought you were through. When everybody else had given up hope and you yourself had given up hope, when nobody else would help, I'm giving you another chance."

I'm a part of the "another chance" crowd. I'm not here because I have always made the right choices. I'm here because morning by morning, God wakes me up and gives me fresh mercy. God gives me another chance. Now, I can make another choice, because an ounce of prevention is worth a pound of cure.

There are some sicknesses we don't have to have. Instead of getting you some red soda, why don't you drink eight glasses of water? Do you have to have swine everyday? Can you, every now and then, just have some turkey bacon?

As a matter of fact, why don't you try going a day just having fruits and vegetables, and get something that is raw and alive, that will give life to your body?

Another chance to make another choice. Jesus healed the man, who is now walking with his bed, and folk had seen him for thirty-eight years, lying down, and they said, "man, what happened?" Now, this man has got to be black, because you know, when you are black, and you can't explain the inexplicable, the typical black response is, "what had happened was…" Everywhere he went somebody said, "man, what happened to you?" Well, "what had happened was": *God so loved the world He gave His only begotten Son that whosoever believeth in Him should not perish but have everlasting life.* "What had happened was": *God was in Christ, reconciling the world to Himself.* "What had happened was": I once was down but now I'm up. "What had happened was": *If any man be in Christ Jesus, he's a new creation, old things are passed away, all things have become new.*

Do I have any "what had happened was" folk reading this, where you can look back over your life and there are some things you just can't explain and so all you can say is "what had happened was" God raised me? "What had happened was" God made a way for me. "What had happened was" God picked me up, turned me around, and placed my feet on solid ground. "What had happened was" I *was sinking deep in sin, far from the peaceful shore; very deeply, stained within, sinking to rise no more.* "What had happened was" *the Master of the sea heard my despairing cry, and from the waters, He lifted me, now safe am I.* "What had happened was" God did the impossible.

When you reach the point when you are sick of being sick, God will step in and do something so miraculous that you can't explain it. So when folk ask you how did you get like you are, just say, "what had happened was…!"

OVER MY DEAD BODY

Rizpah daughter of Aiah took sackcloth and spread it out for herself on a rock. From the beginning of the harvest till the rain poured down from the heavens on the bodies, she did not let the birds of the air touch them by day or the wild animals by night. When David was told what Aiah's daughter Rizpah, Saul's concubine, had done, he went and took the bones of Saul and his son Jonathan from the citizens of Jabesh Gilead. (They had taken them secretly from the public square at Beth Shan, where the Philistines had hung them after they struck Saul down on Gilboa.) David brought the bones of Saul and his son Jonathan from there, and the bones of those who had been killed and exposed were gathered up.

They buried the bones of Saul and his son Jonathan in the tomb of Saul's father Kish, at Zela in Benjamin, and did everything the king commanded. After that, God answered prayer in behalf of the land.

—2 Samuel 21:10-14

What do you do when life has beaten you down so much so that you are at your breaking point? I don't care how long you have been going to church, how big your Bible

175

is, or how much you love Jesus, every now and then, life will push you so close to the edge that you feel you are about to lose your mind. Every now and then, life will break you down and leave you feeling completely shattered.

There is the pressure of going to work and catching hell on the job. There is the pressure of having mounting bills and little income. There is the pressure of dealing with family drama. There is the pressure of dealing with racism and/or sexism. There is the pressure that comes from just waking up in the morning and having to deal with the problems that come from living in this thing we call life. And every now and then, life will break you down to the point where you will say, "you know what? I have had it up to here, I can't take it any more." You may have gone through so much hell that you have reached your breaking point.

Whenever you reach your breaking point, understand that God is so amazingly good that in His grace, He will give you just what you need every single day. As a matter of fact, the writer wrote, *"morning by morning, new mercies I see."* Every day you wake up, God greets you with fresh mercies, knowing that yesterday's mercy is not going to be enough to handle today's challenges. When you think about it, as you look back over your life, if it had not been for the mercy of God, you should have been dead a long time ago. But guess what? If you had known back then what you are about to go through, you would have said, "forget this, I can't handle that." But now, as you are going through it, every morning God gives you just enough peace, just enough strength, just enough grace, and just enough mercy to make it through each day.

Here is what God said to Paul when He allowed Paul to reach his breaking point because of the thorn in his flesh: "I am not going to answer your prayers the way you want Me to. Here's what I'm going to do: I'm going to give you just enough grace, and My grace is going to be so sufficient that My strength is going to be made perfect in your weakness." God says, "when you've reached your breaking point, when you feel as though you can't go on any more, that is when My strength steps in." God gives you strength to go through your situation, and before you know it, somebody is asking, how did you go through that and not lose your mind? God gave you just what you needed to get through what you were going through. God is saying, "when you reach your breaking point, don't break down, break out."

Once I bought some dough biscuits and guess what I discovered? They come in a container and the only way to get the biscuits out is you have to hit the container, and when you hit it, the biscuits pop out. But guess what the dough said to me? The dough said, "you see, I was in my container which was my comfort zone, but my creator did not make me to stay in my comfort zone. My creator recognized the only way to set me free from where I was comfortable was to hit me, and once I got hit, I had to break out of what I was locked into." Realize that when God hits you, God allows you to break out, and not break down.

Besides our own personal issues, understand when you look at all the hell we catch in the hood—when you look at the crime, the violence, and the economic dysfunctionality—those things can cause you to break down. Recently, two children got shot at one of our local high schools—things like that will break you down. When you see the proliferation of guns, gangs and drugs in our community, things like that will break you down.

Father Michael Pfleger, pastor of the Faith Community of Saint Sabina in Chicago, blessed me in a powerful way. He told a story about the fact that the Chicago River, for years, fed Lake Michigan, and Lake Michigan was also a source of drinking water for the residents of Chicago. The Chicago River became polluted, and consequently, much of the drinking water of Lake Michigan became contaminated and this caused people to get sick. The city founders came together and said, what can we do? A scientist said, "the only way you're going to preserve the drinking water in Lake Michigan is you have to somehow reverse the current, because as long as the current is going in the wrong direction, it's going to carry pollutants into your drinking water, and it's going to jack-up people's lives."

Do you not know when you look at the proliferation of

crime and violence in our communities, all that is, is sewage and contamination that has come from a current— a flow of economic injustice, poverty, and racism—and those things have carried all of this sewage into our community? I am hoping that somebody, today, would dare to take a stand and say, "we've got to reverse the current. We do not have to have all these guns in our community."

Now some of you NRA people are saying, "oh, no, Pastor Haynes, guns don't kill people; people do." You are right. But it's people with guns who kill people. What I am trying to figure out is, why do we need all of these guns? Where do these guns come from? How is it that our kids have access to these guns? These guns that are coming into our community are sewage, and we must reverse that current that is coming into our community. We do not own one single plane that flies from South America into this nation, yet look at all the drugs in our community. There is a multinational drug cartel that has inroads into our community because of their connection to corporations in this nation. That is sewage that is keeping all of this negativity flowing into our community.

With all of that sewage, with all of that negativity, with all of that poverty, someone must stand up and declare, "I am going to change the current. I am not going to break down or melt down. I am going to step up and I am going to break out. I am not just going to let stuff happen, I am going to rise up and make things happen. I don't just go to church to sit, look, sleep, and leave; I go to church on Sunday to get some power, so I can go in the community on Monday, and be used by God to reverse the current."

When you look at the proliferation of crime and violence, we see more black folk being affected by crime than anybody else. In so many instances, at the other end of that gun, there is some one that looks just like us. Cain is killing Abel in our community. Because of this proliferation of crime and violence, it is breaking our village, and because of this, somebody must say, I am going to stand up and I am going to speak out. I am going to do what is necessary to make sure that we reverse this current.

Our text is tragic, and yet out of this tragedy there is a bright spot of hope—a bright spot of hope from this sister by the name of Rizpah.

Bible readers, recognize, by way of context, that we begin this chapter with David inquiring of the Lord as to why there is famine in the land. That simply means that in spite of their hard work, they had nothing to show for it; in spite of them giving their best, life was not giving it back to them. There were no jobs. There was no healthcare.

I love what Old Testament scholar, Dr. Walter Brueggemann does. Walter Brueggemann begins to argue with the text, and he says, "When you look at the text, the only one who knows what the Lord says to David is

David himself. The Lord said to David, the reason there is famine in the land is because of the blood on the hands of Saul." Now, Saul is dead, and Walter Brueggemann maintains that the writer of this section wants to make David look good, even though his administration is doing something bad. It's called political propaganda. Political propaganda says, "even when the war is wrong, somehow we got to have a propaganda machine that markets this message—if you do not support the troops then somehow, you are unpatriotic and anti-American."

Howard Dean, head of the Democratic National Committee, came to Dallas and asked to meet with me. Now, I have to be me no matter who I'm meeting with. And so I said to him, "I do not understand why the Democratic Party and Congress buckle under the pressure of the Bush administration. The war could have been ended had they just had enough backbone and not funded this war. Why did you all not stand up against the President? After all, when we swept you into Congress in November, we swept you in, based on your ending this war. We all know it's unjust, it's ungodly, it's unethical, and it's immoral. Folk are dying every day who don't need to be dead, both American and Iraqi. I want to know why you let that man off the hook? Why did you let him do that?"

He agreed with me, and then he said, "It is because we did not just buckle under, but we fell to the propaganda machine because the machine basically had us believing if we did not do this, we were not supporting the troops."

I said, "Support the troops? Here's how you support the troops: bring them home from that war. And when they get home make sure that they have veteran's benefits."

The propaganda machine does not let you know that veteran's benefits have been cut, while the cost of the military has been raised.

So there is the David propaganda machine. The Bible says that the machine is led to believe there is some blood on the hands of Saul. But, there is nothing in the text that says that David had to go kill the remaining relatives of Saul. But, understand, by way of cultural context, that whenever a new blood line assumed the throne, the first order of business was to kill off all of the former king's relatives, so no one from the former king's family could have a claim on the throne. And so, David uses religion to justify his political military maneuvering. The Bible says they go after Saul's family in retaliation. It's a retaliation drive by, and they kill five of Saul's grandsons and two of Saul's sons birthed through his concubine, Rizpah.

The Bible lets us know that as soon as that takes place, they leave the dead, decaying bodies of Rizpah's sons and Saul's grandsons out in the open. As soon as Rizpah gets word of what's going down she says, "no, no, no. Over my dead body!" Do you see the picture? It's a mother crying because her sons are dying.

We read in verse ten: **Rizpah daughter of Aiah took sackcloth and spread it out for herself on a rock. From the beginning of the harvest till the rain poured down from the heavens on the bodies, she did not let the birds of the air touch them by day or the wild animals by night.** Rizpah, this heart-broken mother who has been pawned by the powers that be; Rizpah, who has been used and misused as a concubine of Saul, soon discovered that, in this world, if you are not careful, people will use you and then have no use for you; people who you do good for will get all they can from you and then once they get it from you, if you ever need them, they are nowhere to be found. Rizpah has been used as Saul's concubine, and now her sons are dead. She has nothing to show for being used and Rizpah finally says, "you know what, I've had it up to here. I'm not going to take any more because the last thing you're going to do is dehumanize the dead bodies of my sons."

Do you see this black mother, as she covers her sons' bones with a cloth? Then she stays out there, day and night, from April until October, and every time some scavenger tries to come and tear away the flesh of her children, she fights them off. Do you see the mama? Here comes a jackal. You better not. Here comes a vulture. You better not. Here comes a wolf. You better not. She fights them all off. Imagine that from April until October! This black mama says, "I've had it up to here. You will not do any more damage to my children. Over my dead body!"

You know what blessed me about this is even though
Rizpah had been pawned, and even though she was a
helpless victim up until now, she gathers all that was in
her and said, "you know what? I don't have to be a victim
any more." If you don't get anything else, leave these pages
with a new mentality that says, "you know what, I do not
have to be a victim any more. I do not have to just take
stuff happening. I do not have to roll over and be
somebody's doormat." Whenever you are a doormat, you
get stepped on, you get dirtied, and then you get left
outside, and they close the door on you. You may even
get thrown away.

Rizpah went from being a pawn to being a queen. Rizpah
went from being a victim to setting the stage for a new
victory. The name *Rizpah*, in Hebrew, means *burning
coal*. Coal is hot; it is on fire. Guess what coal that is on
fire and under pressure becomes? A diamond. When there
is enough fire and pressure, what was an ordinary, ugly
piece of coal, all of a sudden becomes a diamond. So all
of a sudden, Rizpah says, "you see, back then, I was just
some coal. I got kicked around. But once I went through
some fire, once I was under some pressure, it brought
out my bling."

God is so good that He can take the bad mess you go
through and use that pressure and fire to bring out your
bling.

How does it work? Let me give you three points:

I. We Can Stop this Epidemic of Crime and Violence

We can stop this epidemic of crime and violence. When you want a helping hand, check out the one at the end of your arm. Quit looking for somebody else to do for you what God has given you the strength, the resources, and the power to do for yourself. God says, "learn to do for yourself." Is that not what Rizpah did? Rizpah said, "nobody is going to be responsible for protecting the dignity of my dead kids, and so I am going to protect their dignity; I am going to cover them. And if it takes months and months of fighting off scavengers, I will do just that, because the power is in my hand."

Coach Eddie Robinson passed away two years ago, and his death reminded me of a story, told by one of his players. They told this story about a football game in which Grambling State University in Louisiana was playing a horrible first half. The first half was just going downhill fast, and soon they came to half time. Eddie Robinson was very upset. The team knew they were in trouble, but the coach did not respond negatively. Instead, he said, "Listen, we are only down by two touchdowns, but we can win this game. Nothing worked in the first half; but something is going to work in this second half, because I have in one of these two boxes the solution to our problem. In one box is the problem as to why we did not do well, and in the other box is the solution. So, I want you, one by one, to file behind these boxes. Then, let's go out and win this game." He said, "When you look in the first box and see the problem, all you have to do is correct the problem by looking in the second box."

So one by one, they looked in the first box—problem. Second box—solution. And then they went out. They turned around that game, and though they went in down by fourteen at the half, they won the game by fourteen, outscoring the opponent by twenty-eight points in the second half.

If you are thinking, "well what was in those boxes?" I will tell you what was in those boxes. The box that said "problem" had a mirror in it. The box that said "solution" had a mirror in it.

When you look at the problems in the black community, look in the box, and there is the problem. Look in the box again and there is the solution. Do you want to be a problem or a solution?

This is what it boils down to: I discovered that Christians are either lampshades or light bulbs. A lampshade looks good, but it does not shed any light. A lampshade is real nice to look at. It may have frills around it, it may have a nice color; but a lampshade does not do anything as far as shedding light in a dark room. But if you want some light, it is not about the lampshade; it is about the light bulb. If the light bulb is connected right, that light bulb can bring light to the dark. God deliver me from lampshade Christians, who just come to church to look churchy, come to church to look holy, or come to church to look good. We need some light bulbs, who are hooked up to Jesus, because when you are hooked up to Jesus, you can light up the world.

Your helping hand is at the end of your arm. We can fight crime if we make up our minds that we are not going to look to anybody else to do it for us.

II. YOUR PERSONAL, PUBLIC DEMONSTRATION CAN RESULT IN POLITICAL AND SOCIAL TRANSFORMATION

The second thing the text makes reference to, which is so powerful, is that **your personal, public demonstration can result in political and social transformation.** Notice verses 11-13: *When David was told what Aiah's daughter Rizpah, Saul's concubine, had done, he went and took the bones of Saul and his son Jonathan from the citizens of Jabesh Gilead. (They had taken them secretly from the public square at Beth Shan, where the Philistines had hung them after they struck Saul down on Gilboa.) David brought the bones of Saul and his son Jonathan from there, and the bones of those who had been killed and exposed were gathered up.* The text says when David heard what Rizpah had done, from April to October—fighting off vultures and jackals—he had a reversal of his public policy, because sometimes, it takes a demonstration that other folk consider extreme. Extreme times call for extreme measures. God deliver me from saints who are just lukewarm, who don't really want to do anything but go to church and be comfortable. That is why if you come to my church, and if all you want to do is hear a word that is going to make you feel good, then you are coming to the wrong place because the world is too deadly, hell is too hot, and black folk are in too much trouble for us to just come to church, sit, shout, and then go on our merry way. We need somebody willing to do something extreme.

Rizpah's act was a demonstration. You may not like demonstrations, but whatever job you work on, it is because somebody demonstrated. Whatever house you live in, it is because somebody demonstrated. Do you not know whatever freedom you have it is because somebody demonstrated? Do you not know that India broke the back of colonialism because Gandhi demonstrated? Do you not know that because Nelson Mandela, Desmond Tutu, Steven Biko, and Winnie Mandela, demonstrated, apartheid was abolished in South Africa? Do you not know because Martin Luther King, Jr., demonstrated, because Medgar Evers demonstrated, and because Rosa Parks demonstrated that there was a change in public policy? Well, maybe what we need to do is leave church one Sunday and demonstrate in the streets that we are not going to take any more crime and violence in our village.

III. You Do All You Can and God Will Handle What You Can't

Finally, the text lets us know **that you do all you can and God will handle what you can't.** You do what's possible for you, and God will handle what's impossible for you. You do your best, and let God handle the rest.

The text says when Rizpah did that, David had all of the bodies buried in dignity. Notice, again, verse 14: *They buried the bones of Saul and his son Jonathan in the tomb of Saul's father Kish, at Zela in Benjamin, and did everything the king commanded. After that, God answered prayer in behalf of the land.* After they were buried in dignity, God heard the prayers of the people, and the famine was over. Why? Because they could not stop the famine themselves; all they could do was do their part, and once they did their part then God said, "now it is on Me to do My part."

One Sunday we were preparing a celebration for the founder of Concord Baptist Church, E.K. Bailey, and that made me look back to when Dr. E.V. Hill's wife had died back in the late '80s. I wanted to go to the funeral to be supportive, and I really did not have the resources then, and so I thought I was not going to be able to make it.

Then E.K. called me and said, "Do you want to go to Dr. Hill's wife's funeral and support, Doc?" I said, "Man, I would like to go, but I really don't have the resources for that kind of trip." He said, "Well, here is what you do: you just get there, and if you get there I will take things from there."

Guess what that meant? That meant getting my plane ticket. Once I got my plane ticket, I got to DFW and Bailey was there. Bailey said, "I have been waiting on you, man; I was hoping you were coming." I said, "Yeah, I was coming." He said, "Well, I was waiting on you because I am going to upgrade you. You bought a coach ticket, didn't you?" I said, "That is all I could afford—coach." He said, "Well, that's why you are with me because I am going to upgrade you. I told you to just get here and I will take things from here."

I rode in first class on a coach ticket because Bailey said, "If you get there, I will take things from there." Can you see me right now—I'm in first class. No, I had not paid for a first class ticket. Some of you are where you are even though you have not paid full price for it; but God said if you get there, I will handle things from there.

This story gets even better. I'm flying in first-class, and the flight attendants came along and served food. I looked in the back where I should have been and said, "Thank you, Bailey, because if I had been in the back, I would not be eating on this plane."

And then, we got to L.A. I said, "Uh-oh, I can't be here homeless. We have to stay overnight." Bailey said, "What did I tell you? You get there, and I will take things from there." When we got to the hotel, Bailey said, "How much do you have?" I said, "I have $100." He said, "Well, keep your $100, so you can eat." He put down his credit card, and when he put down his credit card, Bailey said, "If you get here, I will take things from here."

I stayed that night and I was able to go to the funeral the next day, and it was all because Bailey said, "If you get there, I will handle things from there." It then dawned on me: is that not what it is like to walk with God? There is a whole lot of stuff I can't handle myself but God says, "just get there and I will handle things from there."

That is what God told Abraham: "Abraham, I know you are an old man, but if you get there and make love to your wife, I will handle things from there." And nine months later, they had Isaac. Moses is down at the Red Sea. God says, "since you are here, I will handle things from here," and He made a freeway through the Red Sea. If you get there, God will handle things from there.

DON'T SET YOUR QUEEN UP TO BE A "HO"

Now there was a famine in the land—besides the earlier famine of Abraham's time—and Isaac went to Abimelech king of the Philistines in Gerar. The LORD appeared to Isaac and said, "Do not go down to Egypt; live in the land where I tell you to live. Stay in this land for a while, and I will be with you and will bless you. For to you and your descendants I will give all these lands and will confirm the oath I swore to your father Abraham. I will make your descendants as numerous as the stars in the sky and will give them all these lands, and through your offspring all nations on earth will be blessed, because Abraham obeyed me and kept my requirements, my commands, my decrees and my laws." So Isaac stayed in Gerar.

When the men of that place asked him about his wife, he said, "She is my sister," because he was afraid to say, "She is my wife." He thought, "The men of this place might kill me on account of Rebekah, because she is beautiful."

When Isaac had been there a long time, Abimelech king of the Philistines looked down from a window and saw Isaac caressing his wife Rebekah. So Abimelech summoned Isaac and said, "She is really your wife! Why did you say, 'She is my sister'?" Isaac answered him, "Because I thought I might lose my life on account of her."

Then Abimelech said, "What is this you have done to us? One of the men might well have slept with your wife, and you would have brought guilt upon us."

So Abimelech gave orders to all the people: "Anyone who molests this man or his wife shall surely be put to death."

—Genesis 26:1-11

I read in the newspaper the sorrowful story of a six-year-old girl whose fifteen-year-old brother was her babysitter. Her fifteen-year-old brother had brought his friends over, against the wishes of his parents, who had gone out for the evening. The little girl said, "I'm going to tell," and he threatened her. After threatening her, he went and got a gun out of his parents' bedroom. The parents did not know that the son knew where the gun was. And while playing with the gun, taunting, teasing, and threatening his sister, the gun accidentally went off, and the fifteen-year-old brother shot his six-year-old sister. There she lay, dying in a pool of blood. Why was she laying there, dying in a pool of her own blood? She was there because her fifteen-year-old brother, who was supposed to protect her, had hurt her.

Isn't it sad, that in too many instances, our sisters have looked to our brothers to protect them, and instead of our brothers protecting them, the brothers have been the source of that sister being hurt and wounded? Picture, if you will, that six-year-old sister lying in a pool of her own blood because her brother found what his parents had left behind. His parents had ignorantly left behind what they should not have left.

Brothers, your whole concept of relating to a sister has everything to do with what you beheld as a child. You have become what you have beheld. That sister in your life is wounded because of what you caught from your parents. If we are not careful, we as a community will find ourselves, over and over again, with sisters who are wounded by brothers who have a dysfunctional and disruptive concept of relating to sisters, simply because that is how they were taught by their parents.

But not only that: understand that this little brother had wounded his sister because he had in his hands power that he could not handle. What is a fifteen year old boy doing with a gun? A fifteen year old boy with a gun in his hands is one who has power that he cannot control. So, there I am, reading this article, and my heart is broken. That article is a sad indictment and illustration of what's going on in the African-American community.

Well, as we deal with that, I hope you recognize where I am going already, because in our text, understand that Isaac has set up his own wife, Rebecca, to be treated like a "ho." It blows my mind that Isaac, a descendant of

Abraham; Isaac, an heir to a promise by Almighty God, mistreated his own wife. She was destined to be a queen, but he put her out there as a "ho." She was destined to be a queen, but he threw her under the bus.

I am concerned about this because this nation was in an uproar because of one sixty-six-year-old racist and sexist, who had the nerve to use the power of his media outlet to throw under the bus some sisters who had had a successful basketball season. But, the area he messed up in was the fact that he was talking about some sisters, who were coached by a queen—a queen with dignity whose players reflected the dignity of their coach. I'm simply trying to say that Imus, a sixty-six-year-old racist and sexist was guilty of doing what this nation has historically done to our African-American women.

I am going to hang out here for a moment, because Imus had the nerve to pick up the cudgel of debate, and instead of being contrite, he decided to be confrontational. Look at Imus as he dares to say that he got what he said from what we say in our community. He said, "what I am saying is no worse, than what they say in the hip-hop community." Then the media had the nerve to pick up on that to ask, "Is there a double standard?"

I believe that was hypocritical of the media because this nation has always played us with a double standard. You can't read the Constitution without seeing a double standard—"We hold these truths to be self-evident that all men are created equal"—and yet they labeled us three-fifths of a human being. That is a double standard. They had the nerve to lift up Patrick Henry who said, "Give me liberty, or give me death!" But Patrick Henry had some slaves when he said that. We have always had a double standard. This is the nation that says, "one Nation, under God, indivisible, with liberty and justice for y'all, not all."

There is a double standard when as a black person, even today, I still have to work twice as hard to get half as much in a world where I am still held back because of the color of my skin. It took a lot of gall and gumption to say this was a double standard. And yet, honesty begs us to come together and huddle as a community. It is time for us to take a look in the mirror at how we are treating and mistreating one another—how we are abusing one another, and how we have sadly, sinfully, and shamefully picked up the legacy of dehumanization and disrespect. We have picked up that legacy, and now, nobody tears us down like we tear ourselves down; nobody talks about us any worse than we do; nobody disses our women any worse than we do; nobody runs us down like we do. And I know some of you are talking back to me right now saying, "aw, man, you just trying to bad mouth hip-hop." I am not bad mouthing hip-hop. Recently, I was watching some old black exploitation movies: "Super Fly," "The Mack," and some others, and I understand that hip-hop has basically gotten what they've gotten from the generation before them. So before you judge the fruit, you need to check the roots. Before you judge those who are children, you have to check out the parents.

Have you heard the story about the parent turtles who were talking about how the baby turtles were walking? They said, "Look at how those children are walking. They ought not to walk like that," only to discover that the baby turtles were walking like the adult turtles. So, before we judge this generation of children, we need to check out what we have done as parents in terms of how we have mistreated and disrespected one another.

I am concerned about how we are dissing and mistreating our own women. Of course, we have extreme examples. You may have heard about the incident where they had the nerve to take an ATM card and swipe one of our sister's behinds. That was dissing our sister. That was disrespectful, demeaning, and dehumanizing. We are treating our queens like "ho's". I am here to say that God wants us to put an end to that, and recognize that since we are God's children, God loves us, and God respects us, then we ought to give that love and respect to one another. Why? Because when you respect yourself, you can't help but to love and respect others. When you have a healthy theology, it will influence your sociology, and then govern your biology.

It is hard for me to know I am loved by God and love God back and then don't love you as you ought to be loved. You see, once I love God right because I know

God loves me, that means I can't help but love you right and treat you right because you are a child of God. I, too, am a child of God, and since that makes us brothers and sisters, I can't mistreat my sister because I don't want to tick off my Daddy.

Understand Isaac has been told by God, in a time of famine, "don't go to Egypt, where I know there is a surplus of food. I want you to stay right here in Gerar." Isaac does just that and God blesses him.

But, the text says, they asked about Isaac's wife. His wife is named Rebecca, and Rebecca is a honey. Rebecca has it going on. I mean the girl is fine. The text lets us know that Rebecca is so fine that when they asked about Rebecca, Isaac does not want to have any trouble, and so Isaac, being a weak, spineless man, puts her under the bus by saying, "listen, she is not my wife; she is just my sister." Isaac just puts her out there, and if somebody wanted to step to this fine sister, the text indicates that they could do that. The Book says, because Isaac and Rebecca had their thing that was so passionate, they began to physically express what they emotionally could not suppress. Isaac began to caress his woman, and love on his woman, and make her feel good.

Abimelech happened to look out his window and saw what was happening, and said, "that can't be his sister. That has got to be his wife." He confronted Isaac about this, and Isaac said, "I'm sorry, I didn't mean to do it. I thought you would kill me." Abimelech said, "man, we could have slept with her because you lied to us, and I am not going to let this happen so we are going to protect you."

The text lets us know Isaac made the mistake of setting up his queen to be treated like a "ho". Brothers, we have got to stop putting our sisters out there. We have to stop putting our sisters under the bus. We have to have respect for ourselves and for our sisters. We have to lift them up and treat them properly, if we want others to lift them up and treat them properly. We have to respect our sisters, and not treat them as "ho's," because if we do, they will not find themselves being dissed and disrespected.

Now, let's go back to the story I related to you at the beginning of this chapter. Of course, the brother called 9-1-1. The ambulance comes to take the girl to the hospital. The good news is, he called his father, and his father met him at the hospital. Why is this good news? Because the six-year-old girl had a rare blood type, a blood type similar to that of the father. The father said, "I already know my girl has a rare blood type. You probably do not have it, but she does have my blood because she's my child, and so you can take my blood, and give my baby a blood transfusion." Guess what: that girl is alive and strong today because her father stepped in and gave her a blood transfusion.

There is a wounded sister reading this book—you have

been wounded by some brother that you thought you could trust; you have been hurt by some brother who did you wrong. All you have to do is call up your Father—"Our Father Who art in Heaven." The good news is, two thousand years ago, He gave a blood transfusion, and "There is a fountain, filled with blood, drawn from Immanuel's vein; and sinners plunged beneath that flood lose all their guilty stains."

Now, you know that brother was feeling guilty. He felt badly about what he had done, and he cried and cried over it. But that six-year-old girl set him free. She turned to her brother and said, "Brother, I know you didn't know any better, and so I am going to forgive you." That fifteen-year-old brother is now a counselor on gang and gun violence in Los Angeles, California, and he tells everybody, "I am doing it because I was set free by the forgiveness of my sister who was set free by the blood from my father."

We need some brothers who will say, "you know what, I have messed up; I haven't done everything I should do, but there is a sister who has forgiven me, because our Father has given her new life."

New life. How does that work? I'm going to give you three points and we're done:

I. God is so Good that when you Walk by Faith your Consequences will Never be Limited by your Conditions

This is for the brothers: Brothers, **God is so good that when you walk by faith, trusting God, your consequences will never be limited by your conditions.** Your consequences, how things end up, will never be confined or defined by your current situation.

The text says there is a famine in the land and in spite of there being a famine in the land, God says to Isaac, "stay here. I'm going to bless you right here. Everything around you looks bad, but I'm going to bless you with goodness in the place of badness. Your current conditions look quite negative, but I'm going to give you consequences in spite of your condition that are unexplainable." See, God is that kind of good, where folks will sometimes look at you and wonder how, in spite of everything they think they know is going on in your life, you still wake up every morning with a smile on your face; you still wake up every Sunday and make your way to the House of Prayer. They know you lost your job, but you still haven't missed a bill. Why? Because God is so good, God never allows your condition to determine your consequences.

Can you say that God has been that kind of good to me? When folk look at what is going on in my life, I really shouldn't be smiling; I really shouldn't have my act together, but somehow I do.

I will never forget a trip I took to Morocco. While in Morocco, I rode a camel for the first time. I also learned that camels can go long distances in a dry desert without water. They say it is because camels have a built-in reserve supply, and the reserve supply in the camel says, "regardless of my condition, I can keep on going when other folk would have passed out by now, because I have a reserve tank of water that somehow keeps on feeding me in the midst of the bad conditions around me."

Do you have some camel in you, when really you should have stopped a long time ago, but somehow God kept feeding you just what you needed, and you kept on going? I mean you should have been down by now, you should have quit by now, you should have lost your crazy mind by now, but God gave you power to keep on going because your consequences are not defined by your conditions.

God says, "Isaac, I'm going to bless you in a famine. Isaac, you're going to be fruitful in a famine. Isaac you are going to have it going on in a bad time." Why? Here it is: Isaac stayed. God orders our steps and our stops because there is always provision even in prohibition. God orders our steps and our stops because only God can use our stops; only God can use what prohibits us to give us something we would not have gotten, had we not been stopped. God says, "you don't have to go to Egypt where there is plenty of food. You stay right here in Gerar where there is nothing because I'm going to stop you, not to stop your blessings, but to set you up for some blessing that you wouldn't have had had I not stopped you."

Only God can use what blocks us to bless us. Only God can use what is taken from us to give something extra to us. Only God can use shut doors to give us dividends we wouldn't have received, had the doors not been shut. Even though God orders your steps, He sometimes will stop you; He sometimes shuts a door. There is a blessing even in locked doors.

I will never forget when my nephew had to do an experiment with some hamsters to study about reproduction. My sister let her son keep one of the hamsters and one day when I was over at her house they were playing with the hamster out on the carpet. The hamster was having a good time. Then it was time for the hamster to go back in its cage because we were leaving the room. When we came back in, the hamster stood up against the cage, thinking that since we were back in the living room, it was time to play.

The hamster was trying to get out the cage because it had been trained to expect the cage door to be open whenever we were in the living room. But this time, the door stayed shut. The hamster is just turning around, standing up, eager to get out the cage, but what the hamster did not know was that my sister had let her German Shepherd in the house, and this dog was hiding around the corner. The German Shepherd, with his ears up, was saying to us, "Let him out. Let him out. Go ahead and let him out." The hamster is upset, and I hear the hamster saying to me, "come on Freddy, we were playing just a little while ago. You opened up the door just a little while ago." But the hamster did not know I had a view that was larger than its view. I could see what was around the corner, and so I kept the hamster in the cage. I said to the hamster, "even though you are going to stay in the cage, I'm going to still feed you." So, I put some food in the cage, and I put some water in the cage. I didn't have to take him out to bless him. I could bless him and keep him right there.

Do you thank God for some closed doors? You wanted to get out but God kept the door closed. For many black men, this picture is ideal—we are always coming up against shut doors. They say, "don't be a black man with confidence; don't be a black man who dares to have your own mind and doesn't try to be white, because this is threatening." Don't listen to all of that. Be a black man who's got backbone and you will threaten everybody else. And consequently, doors will shut in your face; but that is when, you have to: *"walk by faith and not by sight,"* and recognize that God can keep some doors closed, and while keeping those doors closed, God can still give you just what you need in the midst of your closed door.

God blessed Isaac because of his ancestors. If you are

conscious of your history, it will determine your date with destiny. Whenever you are conscious of where you come from, it orders your steps where you are because you already know where you are going. Whenever you are conscious of your "rootage," it sets the stage for your "fruitage." God says, in effect, "Isaac, I'm going to bless you because of your daddy. I'm going to bless you because of your past. If you are conscious of what you've been through, then there is a certain way you will carry yourself right now."

That is why I am dealing with the brothers right now, because evidently, whenever we call our sisters out of their name, we're not conscious of our history. Do you not know that this nation has a history of treating our Sisters like "ho's" and "b's"?

I read something that to this day still messes me up and I have to pray about this thing often. There was a sister, who was blessed amply, as Africans are, in terms of what she had "behind" her. She had a "great future behind her," and thus she had something in front of her, and so that past behind her and what she had in front of her, caused white folk to be blown away because they were used to matchstick bodied women. In 1810, they took this sister, who they named Hottentot, all the way to England as a part of a traveling circus. They set her up as a sex freak, and from that moment on, black women began to be seen as sex objects and as things to be toyed with.

And so, black men, we have to recognize, historically, our sisters, have been dissed by white men and seen as sexual objects to be misused. How many black men can remember, as you look back in history, those brothers who were married who had to stand helplessly on the sidelines as their woman was raped, sexually abused, and misused by that white master? No, we cannot call her a "ho"; no, we cannot mistreat her—she is the daughter of Queen Nzingha, she is the daughter of Queen Candice, she is the daughter of Queen Nefertiti.

So I say to all of you daughters of Candace, Nzingha, and Nefertiti: remember what my sister, Kizzy, in the movie *Roots*, did after she had been raped by her own master, and gave birth to her child named George—she raised him in the tradition of her daddy, Kunta Kinte, the Mandingo warrior. Raising him in that fashion, after she was raped, gave her the strength to get up off that bed of humiliation and rise again. That is why I say to every sister reading this book—Rise up Sojourner! Rise up Harriet! Rise up Nanny Helen Burroughs! Rise up India Arie! Rise up Mary J. Blige! Rise up! You're not a sex object! You're not a wench! You're not a "ho"! You are a queen, and you are worthy of being treated as such!

II. If our Sisters are to be Healed and Empowered, we must Reclaim and Rename them as Queens

I'm coming to sisters now. The text indicates that Isaac threw Rebecca under the bus. When Isaac threw her under the bus, Isaac was confronted by Abimelech. Abimelech teaches all of us: **if our sisters are to be healed and empowered, we must reclaim and rename them as queens.** Reclaim them and rename them! Isaac said you are my sister and not my queen. She was almost treated according to how she was named, and left unclaimed.

I read this fiction story about these kids who had rich parents, and the mother had a lot of diamonds. The little boys went to get mama's diamonds and began to shoot marbles with her diamonds. Because they were little boys, they didn't know the value of a diamond. I relate that story to you, sisters, because whenever you mess with a boy, he is going to treat your diamonds like marbles. I am sorry to go here, but boys play games; boys play with toys; boys are not about respecting, they are about conquering; boys aren't about a relationship of mutual respect; a boy simply wants to play games with your diamonds. A boy will underestimate your value, and then treat your diamonds as marbles.

Can I show you how Isaac did that? The text says Isaac started physically messing with Rebecca, so he wouldn't claim her. He wanted to get the goods without being good. Isaac wanted to have physical satisfaction without satisfying her emotionally, without satisfying her spiritually, without satisfying her intellectually. Understand, sisters, when all you do is basically give up the goods without allowing him to treat you good, then you've converted your own diamonds into marbles.

Because of how you are wired, it's dangerous to keep physically doing something that has no emotional, spiritual, and intellectual benefits. If all you are doing is surrendering your physicality, and you aren't getting anything from it spiritually, emotionally, and intellectually, then the sad thing is you have reduced your own value. So quit calling yourself a diamond, when you are nothing but a marble. I'm just being real with you, because women are wired to receive; men are wired to proactively give.

It's kind of like a socket and a plug: a socket receives, and if it receives the right connection, it can light up a room; it can turn on something that hasn't any power. There is nothing like the right socket. Sisters, you have to guard against allowing too many plugs to get in your socket because if too many plugs get in your socket, you can get overloaded and have a power failure. Oh, brothers, so you will know that I am about equal opportunity, if you put your plug in too many sockets, you are going to end up getting electrocuted.

So, Isaac put Rebecca out there. Now Abimelech said, "she is not your sister, she's your wife. You've got to reclaim her, and you've got to rename her." Whenever you know who you are, nobody else can tell you who you are, and you do not have to live down to what other people think of you. As a matter of fact, once you know who you are, you will quit tripping on what other folks think about you. It isn't what they call you that is important. It's what you answer to.

Reclaim and rename who you really are because when you reclaim and rename who you really are, you begin to carry yourself in light of who you really are. Who are you really? You are the head and not the tail. Who are you really? You are the top and not the bottom. You are a child of the King. Who are you really? You are bought with a price. You are a special treasure, God's chosen generation, a royal priesthood. Stop living according to who you are not, and live according to who you are. If you carry yourself like a queen, nobody can treat you whorishly. Carry yourself like the queen that you are.

Some of you may be thinking right now, "Freddy Haynes, you don't understand. I don't know what a queen looks like. I have not seen a queen. My daddy beat my mama. My daddy abandoned my mama. My daddy mistreated my mama. So I don't know what a queen looks like or how a queen should be treated. You're telling me something that sounds good, but it is foreign to my reality. You are trying to give me something that I have never seen before."

Let me tell you something—just because you have not seen it does not mean you cannot be it. I have discovered that God is so amazingly wonderful that He will give you a vision beyond what you have seen to what you have not seen, and you begin to call things that are not as though they already are. I'll give it to you like this: Al Sharpton shouted me when he said, "You know what blew me away when Ray Charles used to sing, 'O Beautiful for Spacious Skies'? Have you thought about that? Ray Charles would sing "America, the Beautiful," and had never seen it. Ray Charles was singing about an America that didn't exist in his framework of reality, but in his lack of eyesight, God gave him insight via foresight, and Ray Charles saw beyond the ugly realities of America in the right now, and God gave him a vision of what America ought to be." Regardless of what has been, God can give you a fresh vision of what ought to be, and when God gives you that vision, that vision will order your steps and change your reality.

The bottom line is, we've got to reclaim and rename. There is power in language. What's killing me now, is that a lot of folk in the hip-hop community are saying stuff like: "That's our reality." "We are simply naming what we see." "We ain't seen nothing but 'ho's' and 'b's.'" "We ain't seen nothing but the 'N' word, so that's our reality, and consequently, we're singing what we see; we are rapping our reality." That is some jacked-up stuff. In rapping their reality, the words "ho" and "b" have become linguistic weapons of mass destruction that are destroying the emotional esteem of our African-American sisters. Why? Because you have sisters who are now trying to rehabilitate those words, and they are wearing those words as badges of honor.

You may even know some sisters who will sit and say, "That's my 'ho'"; "That's my 'b'"; "Yeah, I'm a b." And they wear that name tag proudly. Understand that there is power in language, because the sad thing is, as you adopt a name, you begin to conform to what that name says. My thing is, if you are going to adopt a name, why don't you adopt the name of "queen," or of "princess"; adopt the name of "royalty," adopt a name that is positive, that uplifts, and does not tear down. Rename and reclaim!

III. GOD BLOWS OUR MINDS BY BLESSING US WITH UNEXPECTED SUPPORT FROM AN UNLIKELY PLACE

After we rename and reclaim, because God is so phenomenal, He blows our minds **by blessing us with unexpected support from an unlikely place.**

Abimelech is ticked and says, "we could have slept with her, as fine as she is; but that would have brought guilt on us, and we don't want any guilt on us, so I'm issuing public policy—that public policy is: nobody molests or messes with Isaac and Rebecca." God does that when we get to the root of where we went wrong because once we get to the root of where we went wrong, we can reap the fruit of things that blow our mind. He says, "Isaac, why did you lie?" Isaac says, "because I was scared."

And that is what we have to get to. We have to get to the root causes of why our boys feel it is all right to call our sisters out of their name. I have already told you that many of them say: "We are rapping about our reality." That is what Russell Simmons makes us think about when he says, "If you want to just talk about the problem, that's fine; but until you deal with the root causes of the problem..." Maxine Waters put it like this: "Don't just talk about the lyrics they are reciting; why don't you talk about the reality that brought about the lyrics they have to recite?"

Why don't you deal with issues of poverty, issues of racism? Why don't you deal with the crack cocaine that somehow got in our community, even though we don't have access to the planes to fly in drugs from Central and South America ourselves? Before you judge the lyrics, you got to deal with the harsh realities. We have to deal with the root causes. And in dealing with the root causes, God will bless us with some fruitful consequences, and the fruitful consequences will come from places we least expected.

God said to Isaac, "I'm going to have Abimelech take care

of you." Don't forget the theme of chapter twenty-six—theologically, it is the theme of blessing. And blessing is not just bling-bling. Blessing has to do with the manifestation of the goodness of God in your situation, in giving you just enough to handle whatever it is that is trying to mishandle you. The blessings of God are the manifestations of the goodness of God that show up just when you need it to give you just what you need; and sometimes, it comes from a source you never would have expected it from.

Yes, who provided Isaac and Rebecca with secret service? It was the Philistines. The Philistines, who were supposed to be their enemies, are the ones who took care of them. Only God can use folk who try to block you to bless you. Only God can use folk who try to stop you, to set you up for what you wouldn't have received had they not tried to stop you.

Can you look back over your life and remember God using some folk who did not plan on blessing you, to bless you? God used some folk who did not plan on doing good to you, to do you good.

Here's what gets me, but gives me hope at the same time. See, even though you are a real child of God, you are not going to always make the best decisions or make the right choices. All of us have missed exits off the Fool's Freeway. All of us have done some stuff we wish we had not done, and have done it with the wrong person, and we have gone to places we wish we had not gone. But, look at God's grace: God says, I am not going to wipe you out. I'm going to set you up. And I'm going to set you up with the very thing that you messed up in.

I had to preach at the Sojourner's Conference in Washington, D.C. I was scheduled to preach on Sunday night, but due to bad weather, I got in late so I was rescheduled for Monday morning. They were having the debate with Hillary Clinton, Barack Obama, and John Edwards that same Monday in the same building as the Sojourner's Conference. Hillary, Barack, and John wanted to come in early to get in on some of the conference. I couldn't get there when I wanted to get there, but I got there when God had me there, and I am so glad that the first door was shut, because Hillary, Barack, and John all had to sit and hear me declare "*thus saith the Lord.*"

After the conference was over, Barack, Hillary, and John all rushed to me, trying to shake my hand. Now, there were some people already in line in front of them, and my thing is, I am not going to treat you better than somebody else because of your position, because at the Cross, the ground is level. There are no big I's and little You's.

There was a brother in front of them who I talked with at length after I preached. He asked could he give me his testimony. So I said, "Yeah, man, go ahead." The brother shared this with me: "You know what, my life is so wonderful right now because I messed up." I said, "Huh?" He said, "Yeah, I messed up big time. I was driving along and I got lost because I made a wrong turn. I just thought I knew where I was going. It turned out I didn't know where I was going. And as a man, I wasn't going to stop and get directions from anybody. So, I kept on going, and kept on going, and kept on going, and then finally, to make matters worse, I ran out of gas. I had to walk to get some gas. I saw a sister walking also, and so I spoke to her. She didn't speak back, and I said, 'Listen, my car ran out of gas. I am going to get some gas.'

"We began to have a conversation. And the conversation got real good. We got to the gas station, and she said, 'Listen, my house is right around the corner. I am going to my house to get my car and I will give you a ride back.' That's how good the conversation was, and by the way, Pastor, if you don't mind, the girl was fine." I said, "Is that right?" He said, "And I was already tore up from the floor up because my heart had been broken last year by a woman who had cheated on me, and now this tenderoni was walking with me. She gave me a ride back to my car. By the way, I had also lost my job. Her daddy owns a corporation, and I met him one week later. By that time, me and his daughter were dating real strong.

"To make a long story short, we met ten years ago and here she is right here." He showed me this fine sister. He said, "This is the woman I met because I made a wrong turn, but I made a wrong turn into my right future. Now I have a good job, now I'm doing well, but it never would have happened had I not made the wrong turn."

I am sure you can testify along with me that the God we serve is so good that even when you make a wrong turn, God can bring a blessing out of that wrong turn. Is there anybody who says, "I'm not going to let nobody treat me less than the God Who made me, because 'can't nobody do me like Jesus? Can't nobody do me like the Lord.' He is my Friend, and because He is my Friend, I'm going to treat you right. Because He is my Friend, I am going to treat myself right." Because He is our Friend, let us never set up our queens to be "ho's".

WHAT HAPPENS WHEN A BLACK MAN GOES HOME

As Jesus was getting into the boat, the man who had been demon-possessed begged to go with him. Jesus did not let him, but said, "Go home to your family and tell them how much the Lord has done for you, and how he has had mercy on you." So the man went away and began to tell in the Decapolis how much Jesus had done for him. And all the people were amazed.

—Mark 5:18-20

It was the third of September.
That day I'll always remember,
'Cause that was the day that my daddy died.
I never got a chance to see him.
Never heard nothing but bad things about him.
Mama, I'm depending on you to tell me the truth.

Do you remember that song? The Temptations went on to testify that as they shared the story of this particular son listening to his mother lament the wasted life of his father, she simply said to the son:

Son, Papa was a rolling stone.
Wherever he laid his hat was his home.
(And when he died) All he left us was ALONE.

What a sad song. But, in reality, it portrayed the plight of too many African-American boys in the '60s and '70s, whose fathers were AWOL (absent without leave) from their lives. Surely, I think we will agree that a part of our brokenness as a village has to do with the absenteeism of African-American men in their families. Statistics reveal that only 33% of our children grow up with fathers in the home. That means a stunning 67% of our black families are headed by unwed, single mothers, and our children are growing up, and finding themselves without the positive, strong, masculine influence of a father.

Now, to park here, parenthetically, let me take off my hat, in symbolic salute, and appreciatively applaud those strong and sagacious sisters who have done the right thing. In a real sense, they have had both the breast of a mother and the chest of a man, as they have attempted to rear their children in the ***"fear and admonition of the Lord,"*** without the positive presence of a masculine influence.

We have, in many instances, sisters who have stepped up, and then we have brothers who find themselves taking charge of a child who does not have their DNA. They recognize that their theology is greater than their biology, and as a consequence, because of their liberated psychology, many brothers have stepped up and they are making a difference in the lives of children that they did not father, biologically.

Yet, I am sure you will agree with me, that too many of our young boys and girls are growing up without that masculine touch, without that masculine influence, and in many instances, it's because "papa was a rolling stone." Many times it is because of irresponsibility on the part of many of our African-American males, and today, my challenge is for us to lift up and hold up the positive models of African-American men who recognize their power when they find themselves at home.

The Power of Presence

One of the things I love to do during the Christmas season is watch those Christmas movies that have so much meaning. Perhaps you recall one particular movie called *Jack Frost*. In this movie, Jack Frost, who is played, I think, by Michael Keeton, is an aspiring musician who wants to blow up. He has huge dreams to one day have a recording contract and utilize his gifts, but, in many instances, he is fulfilling his dream to the neglect of his eleven year old son, Charlie.

In one particular moving scene, he misses his son's hockey game. Charlie is devastated and disappointed because daddy was not at the game. Why? Because Charlie recognized what all children recognize, and that is that children spell "love"—"T-I-M-E." In many instances, fathers who have been absent and who have missed significant time with their children try to make it up with presents or gifts; but there is no gift like your presence.

In this movie, Jack finds himself absent without leave at significant times in the life of his eleven year old son. One day, he decides to make it up to Charlie. Recognizing the power of presence, he says to Charlie, "This Christmas, we are going to get away, and we are going to have a good time, in a cabin, up North in the mountains. We are going to have a good time as a family." Charlie is excited with the expectation that Daddy is going to spend time with him.

But then, the phone call comes. (Isn't it amazing that when you would do good, something comes up that, in a real sense, tests what it is you have decided to do that is good?) A recording company calls to tell Jack, "Here is a contract, but you've got to fulfill an obligation, and play on Christmas morning."

What is Jack to do? He has made a promise, but this is his breakthrough. This will set his career up. He is a man who wants to fulfill his dream. He is a man who wants to provide for his family. And now, he is at a crossroads: does he spend Christmas with his family and fulfill a promise? Or does he spend Christmas fulfilling his dream so he can provide for his family?

There is a brother right now, like you, at the crossroads. You understand the dilemma of the decision that Jack found himself facing in that you want to do right by your family, but as a man, you want to be able to provide for your family. As a man, you want to be able to look in the mirror and know that you are doing the right thing, but it causes you too often, to break promises to your children, and to your family.

Jack then talked with his wife and they come up with a plan. The plan is, Jack is going to spend the morning of Christmas playing with his band, and then rush back to be with his family that night. Well, you know, their compromise is devastating to Charlie. Charlie can't handle or understand the compromise. After all, Daddy, you promised.

Some of you have probably experienced too many moments in your own childhood where Daddy promised but a promise was broken, your dream was deferred, and your heart was broken. That is where Charlie is in the movie. Jack is driving to the place where he is going to perform in the concert, but while driving, all he can think about is how this is negatively impacting his child. He makes up his mind that it is much more important for him to keep his promise as a father than it is for him to fulfill his dream as a musician. When the right deal comes along, it is going to be at the right time, and it is going to be right for everybody involved. Every now and then, you have to recognize that it is best to *"seek first the*

Kingdom of God," and then trust God to do what you can't do yourself.

Charlie finds out that Jack makes a U-turn, and he is heading back home. In a blinding snowstorm and with the windshield wipers not working, Jack crashes, and is killed. What a tragic end.

But then a year later, if you have seen the movie, Charlie is outside doing what he and his father used to do together—he is building a snowman. And in the process of building a snowman, the spirit of his father, Jack, gets into the snowman. This is where the cartoon, "Frosty the Snowman" comes in. The spirit of Jack is in the snowman, and Charlie is excited because his father is back, and Charlie is escorted, after a day of playing with his father, into his bedroom. Frosty kisses his son good night, and as he does that, tears flow out of his eyes as he says, "I spent all of my life trying to make my mark on the world," and then he goes quiet and says to his son who is now asleep, "you are my mark on the world".

Let me say to every black man reading this that your mark on the world is not the job that you have; it is not the house that you live in; but the mark you are going to leave on the world is what you do in the life of the child God has blessed you with. So, brothers, we have to leave our mark on the world, and the mark that we leave has everything to do with what we do in the lives of our children.

Some brothers are saying, "well, Pastor Freddy, you don't know how hard it is for me to go home. You don't recognize the conditions I find myself in as a black man in this white-controlled world."

Let me relate to you another movie I watched, "A Time to Kill," starring Samuel L. Jackson. In that movie, his daughter is brutally gang-raped by some vicious racists. This is what she said to her father when he comes in to the emergency room, and sees her badly broken and bruised: "Daddy, I kept calling for you, but you weren't there. Daddy, I kept calling for you. Where were you, Daddy?" Samuel L. Jackson was living in a racist society that precluded him from answering the cries and call of his daughter.

It dawned on me while reflecting on that movie, that shortly after slavery, in the early 1900's, statistics say that 95% of all black families were headed by African-American males. By 1920, 85%, or 6 in 7 of black homes, were headed by black men. Sadly, today, only 33% of our families are headed by African-American males. What has gone wrong in our broken village? I am here to say that something has happened. Maybe our text will provide some clues that will let us know what has happened in our broken village where too many of our papas are "rolling stones," too many of our children are crying out as they are brutalized by society, "Daddy where are you? Where were you? I cried for you, but you never did come."

Well, at the beginning of our text, by way of context, this demon-possessed man was away from home. The Bible says that because of his own personal demons, he was incarcerated, internally, with his own issues. Sometimes a brother is away from home because of his own demons that he is dealing with. Not only that, while away from home, society can't control him, and so they try and lock him up, because that is always the solution that society tries on African-American men.

They don't know what to do with us, and so they have an unjust criminal justice system that continues to lock us up. Isn't it shameful that in Dallas the Innocence Project has discovered that no other city in the nation leads like Dallas in convictions that have been overturned by DNA evidence? That means there has been a rush to judgment. In too many instances, those who have been in prison are African-American males who have lost twenty plus years because of a rush to judgment because they did not have Johnny Cochran to say, "If it does not fit, then you must acquit." They did not have adequate representation. In too many instances, they had to settle for attorneys who were court-appointed attorneys, and court-appointed attorneys are already overloaded. Many times, they are unfamiliar with the case that they have to argue. Black males are often absent from the home because a system that does not know what to do with them decides to lock them up.

The man in our text has his own personal demons, and

the Bible says Jesus shows up in town. That is my Good News of the Gospel today: every now and then, the Lord will show up. And when the Lord shows up, I promise you, you will never leave the same.

Let me give you three points, because the text says Jesus showed up, and when the brother went home, it changed a whole lot of things.

I. When a Black Man goes Home, it is because of the Difference in His Life, because of the Deliverance he has Experienced from that which Disconnected Him from Home in the First Place

The text lets us know that **when a black man goes home, it is because of the difference in his life, due to the deliverance he has experienced from that which disconnected him from home in the first place.** You see, whenever the Lord makes the difference in you, it is because He delivered you from that which had disconnected you from home in the first place. Whenever the Lord makes a difference in you, He deals with the demons in you, and then delivers you from them, so you can be what God intends you to be.

You can literally divide this man's life into B.C. and A.D.— B.C.—before Christ; A.D.—after deliverance. B.C., before

Christ, he was mad; A.D., after deliverance, he was glad. B.C., before Christ, he was out of his mind; A.D., after deliverance, he was in his right mind. B.C., before Christ, he was confused; A.D., after deliverance, he was clear. B.C., before Christ, he was miserable; A.D., after deliverance, he was a man with a mission. B.C., before Christ, he was naked; A.D., after deliverance, he was clothed. B.C., before Christ, he was crazy; A.D., after deliverance, he was crazy for Jesus. B.C., before Christ, he was a fool; A.D., after deliverance, he was faithful. Can you look back over your life and see where God has bisected your life, and your life is divided into B.C. and A.D.?

Jesus changed this man's life. And that is my word to some brother today—the Lord will change your life. You do not have to be what you have been, you do not have to do what you have been doing, and today can be the first day of the rest of your life. Why? Because God will deliver you today from that which disconnected you from your home to begin with.

Some of you brothers might be thinking, "see Pastor Freddy, I am in church. That means I'm at home." A lot of folk don't realize that you can be absent in your presence. A lot of men think that because they are physically present that that is all that is required. You can be physically present, but emotionally absent. The O'Jays sang it like this: "Your body's here with me, but your mind is on the other side of town." Let's put it like this, just because you are there physically, it does not mean you have a spiritual presence.

This brother was disconnected from his home, and Jesus delivered him, and in delivering him, Jesus said you have to name your pain if you are going to reclaim your name. I'm telling you, if you don't deal with your pain, you won't be delivered from it. Until you confront your pain, you will not conquer it. Until you face your pain, you will not be free from it. Jesus says to the man, "what's your name? Say your name, because your problem is your name issue." The man says his name is "Legion."

Legion was a battalion of Roman soldiers, numbering 6,000. He says, "my name is Legion, because it is so many of us in here." I don't know about you, but have you thought about the fact that in you is more than just you? There are, a lot of times, because of some other influences in you that, when you would do good, evil is right there. Have you ever been in church, knowing you were here to praise God, and a thought just jumped in your head that was totally contrary to your desire to praise God? It's because there is a whole lot of stuff in you that is contrary to you. So, Jesus says, "say your name."

Dr. Obery Hendricks, a brilliant African-American New Testament scholar, who practices what he calls *Guerrilla Hermeneutics* (in which he goes into a text and engages the text by checking out the context, because a text out of context will cause you to get conned) said, "You've got to realize Mark is writing to Roman Christians, and in writing to Roman Christians, Mark uses some symbolism." Don't forget, Legion had to do with Roman occupational forces, which were occupying and oppressing those who were in the land. So he says, "My name is Legion because I've got Rome in my head. I've got the oppressor in my head. The reason I can't be what I am supposed to be, the reason I am engaged in self-destructive behavior, the reason I am engaged in self-hatred and doing that which is contrary to my own interests is because I've got too much of Rome in my head." Have you ever thought about why black folk will do stuff that is contrary to their own interests? It is because we have Rome in our heads.

And so Jesus says, "say your name." Your real name is who you really are. I read this story about this lion that was a part of this circus. One day, when the lion tamer cracked his whip, the lion turned on the trainer, and chased the trainer out of the cage. That trainer, never again, came into that cage with that particular lion. Because of that they set the lion free on a game reserve in Kenya, and a commentator puts it like this, "That lion finally awoke to what he really was, the king of the jungle, and not a toy to be played with, and once the lion realized who he was made to be, he wasn't going to be toyed with anymore."

I believe I am writing to some black man who needs to recognize that once you name your pain and reclaim your name, you are going to realize the lion in you that God made you to be; and since God made you a lion, "king of the jungle," you will never allow anybody to play with you as a toy, and tame you out of something that God made you to be, because you know who you are. When you wake up to who you are, you won't let people treat you other than who you are.

II. YOU HAVE TO GET RID OF THE PIGS

Name your pain, but after you have named your pain, **you have to get rid of the pigs.** Notice the text: *And he begged Jesus again and again not to send them out of the area. A large herd of pigs was feeding on the nearby hillside. The demons begged Jesus, "Send us among the pigs; allow us to go into them." He gave them permission, and the evil spirits came out and went into the pigs. The herd, about two thousand in number, rushed down the steep bank into the lake and were drowned.* In other words, the demons said to Jesus, "please, please don't dog us." Jesus said, "Where do you want to go?" They replied, "to the pigs." Here is my question to you: What are pigs doing in a kosher environment? This isn't South Dallas, where you have BBQ stands available everywhere. No, no, no, this is a kosher community with swine. What are swine doing in a kosher community?

Dr. Johnny Ray Youngblood answered this question when he said, "This represents an underground economy." This represents an economy of hot goods (such as crack cocaine), because wherever there is oppression and dysfunction, there is always an underground economy—

an economy of stuff that is not helpful to the community, but which represents the economic dysfunctionality in that community.

Jesus sends the demon out of the brother into the swine, and then the swine drown in the lake. So, Jesus not only sets this brother free from the inside out, but He deals with the community dysfunction around Him when he says, "we've got to get rid of the pigs."

Now, here's the danger. The text says: **When they came to Jesus, they saw the man who had been possessed by the legion of demons, sitting there, dressed and in his right mind; and they were afraid** (Mark 5:15). As long as this man was acting the fool, cutting himself, screaming, making all kinds of noise; as long as he was calling women "B's" and "Ho's"; as long as he was doing that which was self-destructive, the people were all right with that. But the moment he is seated at the feet of Jesus, dressed right, ain't sagging, and in his right mind, the text says that they were scared. There is nothing this nation fears more than a black man who is clothed, in his right mind, and hooked up with Jesus.

Next, the text says that the man who had been demon-possessed says to Jesus, "let me go with You. I want to kick it with You. You did this for me; I want to stay with You." But Jesus says, "no." After the man is delivered from that which disconnected him, he experiences the Lord saying no that he might say yes to a greater calling.

It was good that this man wanted to be with Jesus. It was noble, in fact. But this was not the Lord's will for him. You may have some noble plans, dreams, and aspirations, but if God has not opened the door for them to come to pass yet, it is because God is saying no. God does not say yes to every prayer request. God does not say yes to everything you want, even if you think it will benefit Him. Sometimes God says no to your requests, because He wants you to say yes to the mission He has for you.

Every now and then, God shuts doors to our dreams because God is trying to point us in a new direction—a direction in which we surrender to a calling that we had not planned on surrendering to in the first place. And if you are wondering whether or not I am in Bible country, ask Moses. Moses, according to Stephen, in Acts 7, had planned on starting a revolution in Exodus 2, when he killed the Egyptian, but God said no and Moses' own people turned on him. Moses spent forty years in the wilderness because God was preparing him to say yes to the mission that God had for him. God may have said no to what you thought you had to have because His assignment for you is greater than you—it is an assignment where God will use you beyond your wildest imaginations.

I have preached in many churches across this nation, but there are three in particular that I am ashamed to even mention their names. The reason why I say that is because they literally bragged to me that Dr. Martin Luther King, Jr., applied to be their pastor and they turned him down. These three churches are not doing anything now, yet they are proud to say "Martin Luther King, Jr., sought to be our pastor, and we turned him down."

I can just imagine how Dr. King must have felt when he applied to such-and-such a church in Oklahoma City, and they told him that we are going to get a better man than you. He must have felt terrible when such-and-such a church in New York City said, no, we are going to call somebody else. But God kept saying no because God knew that down in Montgomery, Alabama, there was a Dexter Avenue Baptist Church, and if King had gone to Oklahoma City or New York City, he would have missed out on an important era in black history, because one year after King arrived at Dexter Avenue Baptist Church, Rosa Parks said, "I ain't taking this mess no more," and refused to stand up. Because she did that, Dr. King, who was turned down by this church and that church became the leader and drum major for justice. Isn't God good like that? God will shut some doors because He has a greater calling on your life.

As some of you may know, I am the co-chair of the Samuel Dewitt Proctor Conference, and we were having our legislative summit in Washington, D.C., where we met with all of the Congressional people, Presidential candidates, and so forth. This particular year, I had a major suite on the top floor of the hotel where we were staying.

When I got to the hotel on Sunday night (I won't forget this as long as I stay black), I was trying to get to my room quickly, because I was broke-down tired. As soon as I got my key from the front desk receptionist, I saw that across the lobby there was an elevator that was getting ready to close. So, I told the receptionist, "Thank you, I have to run." She said, "Hold on." And I told her, "I will talk to you later." I ran on as best I could, trying to get to the elevator before it closed, and I shouted to the person, "Hold the elevator, please." But they just started laughing at me, and the elevator door shut.

Now, to say the least, I was ticked because they were white people, and I don't play that kind of mess. So, I said to myself that I was going to watch to find out what floor they got off on because I was going to go up there and let them know that I don't play that. Then, the front desk receptionist said, "Dr. Haynes, Dr. Haynes." I said, "What?" She said, "That elevator doesn't go to your floor. That elevator only goes to the seventh floor, and you are on the top floor. I am glad you did not get on that elevator, because if you had, it would not have taken you where you were meant to go."

Can you look back over your life and thank God for some closed doors? Thank God we do not always get everything we think we ought to have, because God knows it isn't going to take us where we are supposed to go.

III. Go Home and Spread the Good News

Jesus says to the man, "no, you can't go with Me. I want you to **go home and spread the Good News**. Go tell your family the good things the Lord has done." And in verse twenty the text says: *"He went and spread the good news in the Decapolis."* "Decapolis" means "ten cities". Brothers, when we go home, God says, "you are going to have so much energy, based on what I have done for you, that you are going to allow Me to work through you to do more than you set out to do."

The whole community was impacted by this brother's transformational testimony; not just his home, not just his family, but the whole community was amazed. That's why I know what Dr. Cain Hope Felder said about this text has to be true. He said, "This is an area inhabited by black folk, and so he had to be black because can't nobody talk like a black man." This man had to be hip-hop, because this is how he answers the folks when they asked him what happened to him: that is what that is—*"For God so loved the world that he gave his one and only Son, that whoever believes in him shall not perish but have eternal life."* That is what that is.—*"Therefore, if anyone is in Christ, he is a new creation; the old has gone, the new has come!"* That is what that is.—*"For the wages of sin is death, but the gift of God is eternal life in Christ Jesus our Lord.*" That is what that is.—Cast your cares upon God because God cares for you. That is what that is.—Can't nobody do me like Jesus. Can't nobody do me like the Lord. That is what that is.

Because of this man's testimony, the people are getting saved, and the beauty of this is that Jesus told him, "no, you are not going to hang with me. You are going back to your community." Brothers, don't get delivered, and then get amnesia. God deliver me from saved, blessed black folk, who get what God has blessed them with and then get amnesia about where they came from. You have to go back to your community because there is some black boy who needs to know that he can go to a school in the hood, and turn out to be good. God deliver me from black folk with amnesia.

Now, this is what gets to me: the man sets out to go home just to his family. But when the Lord changes you, you get some energy where you can't just tell one person; you can't just tell the folk in your house; you can't just tell this person or that person; it's like everywhere you go, you are going to let your light shine.

God is so good that you will set out to do one thing, but God will use you to do that one thing and a whole lot of other things as well. All Frederick Douglass wanted to do was escape from slavery, but he ended up becoming the silver-tongued orator of the liberation struggle of abolitionists for African-Americans. All Nelson Mandela wanted to do was fight apartheid in South Africa, but Nelson Mandela went from being prisoner to president of the First Republic of South Africa, and now he is a world-renowed elder statesman. Martin Luther King, Jr., just wanted to pastor a little church down in Montgomery, Alabama, but God had bigger plans for him. That is all I am saying—even if God is saying no to what you thought you had to do, when God says yes He will give you a whole lot more than what you set out to accomplish. Can you testify that you set out to do one thing, but God used you to do a whole lot more?

The Apostle Paul says it best in Ephesians 3:20: "***Now unto him that is able to do exceeding abundantly above all that we ask or think, according to the power that worketh in us.***" It simply means that sometimes God will do things for you that you didn't pray for, you didn't ask for, and you never thought about.

Sometimes God may say no to what we want because He has a different plan that He wants us to say yes to. When you go home, you may set out to do just one thing, but God is a "more than" God, and He gives us the grace and strength to do more than what we set out to do. If you're honest, you will admit that if God had just answered your prayers like you specifically stated, you wouldn't be all that you are right now.

You have come to the end of this book, and if you know

good and well that you are not saved, that you are not a Christian, and you know that there is a whole lot of stuff in you that you need deliverance from, and that is hijacking your hopes, hindering your plans, and causing you to get in the way of you, may I encourage you to give your life to Christ? The beauty of it is, God has a whole lot that He is up to in your life. God has a mission for you. God has plans for you. God is up to something big in your life. You may want one thing, but God may have a whole lot more for you.

If you're not saved, please don't hesitate to give your life to Christ. The Lord is speaking to you. The Bible says: *"The day you hear God's voice, harden not your hearts."* You may ask, "preacher, how do I know God is speaking to me?" You know. Your conscience is being messed with right now. Something inside of you is saying, "you ought to give your life to Christ." That's God speaking.

Since God is speaking, here's the deal: you have a choice to make: you can choose to stay right where you are and allow things to stay the way they are, or you can make the choice to go the other way. If you do what you've been doing, you are going to keep getting what you've been getting. But here's the good news: today, you can make the choice to go the other route. You can experience a new life, a fresh start, a new beginning simply by giving your life to Christ.

1555519

Made in the USA